WHAT A GOOD IDEA!

ACTIVITIES for children in the church

A Co-operative venture by The Joint Board of Christian Education (Australia) and
The National Christian Education Council

Adapted from *What a Good Idea* by permission of the publisher, The Joint Board of Christian Education,
Second Floor, 10 Queen Street, Melbourne 3000, Australia

Designed by G Nicholls

Cover by Jennifer Richardson

Published by:
National Christian Education Council
Robert Denholm House
Nutfield
Redhill
Surrey RH1 4HW

British Library Cataloguing-in-Publication Data:
What a Good Idea
 I. Trenaman, David R.
 262.15

ISBN 0-7197-0784-6

Printed and bound by Halstan & Co Ltd, Amersham, Buckinghamshire HP6 6HJ

CONTENTS

INTRODUCTION

Children come to the church open and smiling, ready to formulate new insights and ideas, as they spend time learning with their leaders and friends. As a leader you have the special task of introducing children to this new and exciting dimension of their life. Children have a lot to offer one another and the church. Answer their questions, accept their marvellous gifts. Make their activities a wonderful beginning to their life of learning and growing in the church.

Through your enthusiastic and creative introduction to the life and teachings of the church, you can help the children to be part of the total church family. Use the following pages to help plan how you will work with the children.

It is important to plan ahead.

- Will you plan around a theme or a special event?

- Are you going to work towards contributing something to a worship time with the church congregation?

- Do you need to arrange for special equipment or resources or help from resource people?

Plan far enough ahead to allow time for children to be excited by what is coming.

Some leaders find it beneficial to plan with a fellow leader, sharing ideas and resources. Draw from each chapter of the book and plan an interesting, challenging programme for the children in your care, using the reading list where necessary for further ideas.

Talking and doing

Children need to explore and think for themselves about the Christian story and its meaning for their lives and for the world. They need to make their own discoveries about the Bible and have experience in expressing themselves and communicating what they believe. How can the leader make this possible? Simply talking to a group of children, even in the tongues of angels, is not enough without love, and love needs to be expressed through some understanding of how children learn. From his experience with Aborigines, Jack Goodluck expresses in a simple verse something about their folk ways of learning through doing, ways that are valid for everyone.

A picture makes it here;
A story makes it clear;
A song makes me feel;
A testimony makes it real;
A chat lets me name it;
A report lets me frame it;
A decision makes me claim it;
A touch makes it here at hand;
A dance lets me join the band.

Jack Goodluck

The Folk Educators

There is so much truth here for us. This chapter is about some of the ways children can be encouraged to share ideas and experiences and take responsibility for their own experience (testimony, chat, report, decision). Other chapters are about the use of pictures, stories, songs, drama and handcrafts (touch the dance in Jack Goodluck's terminology).

Free play for little children

Activities for young children need to be broken up into short interesting segments, with plenty of time for play.

Playing together, children learn how to get on with one another; they are helped to overcome shyness. They see the leader as a friend who also likes to play. They regard the group as a place where their needs and feelings are taken seriously. Physical skills are developed and information gained in story time and worship is assimilated and developed through play. Social skills grow through make-believe games.

An area for the young children could include:

Housekeeping corner

Have an area divided from the rest of the room equipped with child and doll-sized furniture such as a pram, bed, stove, table and chairs. Dress-up clothes, telephones and tea sets encourage dramatic play and help the children explore many aspects of life.

Sand pit — Indoor or outdoor.

Keep the sand clean and slightly moist. Provide moulds, small cars, boats, dolls etc.

Water Play

Water relaxes tension, uses surplus energy and gives great pleasure to children. They like painting outside walls with water, sailing small boats, pouring through funnels, squeezing sponges. Provide large shallow bowls of water, plastic equipment and plastic aprons.

Books & Puzzles

Picture books, simple jigsaw and inset puzzles, construction toys, large beads for stringing and similar materials are particularly useful for those who come early. Arrange them on a shelf or low table for children to make their own selection.

Block Corner

Have blocks of all shapes and sizes. Odd shaped builder's offcuts can be sanded smooth; boxes and cartons can be stuffed with newspaper and covered with coloured paper. A rug on the floor helps to absorb noise. Small cars and trucks add interest to block play...

Using free space and time

Handcrafts, drama, books and walks can provide relaxed times with a leader for talking, sharing and responding to each others ideas.

Books and Games

Have interesting books available for the children's free reading and browsing. Commercially made games or games made by the children can provide fun in spare moments.

Bible reading and prayer

When a child expresses interest in deepening his or her Christian understanding and experience, an aware leader can give encouragement, without trying to control this movement of the Spirit. Such an interest is more typical of teenagers. However, simple and attractive guides to private Bible reading and prayer for younger children are available and can be recommended. Ask at bookshops about publications of the International Bible Reading Association.

Discussion

Even before they talk properly, children enjoy a chat. It is important for children and adults as well to pay respectful attention to the experiences and opinions of others. As they grow, children are increasingly able to put their ideas into words and listen to others.

A discussion is something more than a casual conversation. It is a conversation with a purpose. Leaders can use discussion to help children clarify their ideas. Consider these aspects of leading a discussion . . .

Children need some *background information* before they can join a discussion. Discussions can best take place after a story, outing, film or other first hand experience.

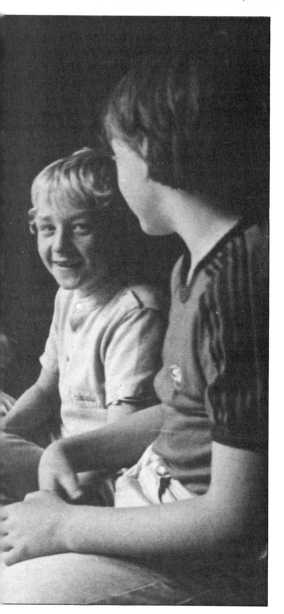

Opening Discussion — Begin with a challenging statement or stimulating question, not one that can be answered with a simple 'yes' or 'no' but something to raise issues or invite the sharing of insight or opinions.

Summary — With older children, and especially if the discussion is to lead to a decision, a brief ongoing summary on chalkboard or paper will help the group. Keep to the point and remember what has been said.

Buzzy groups — Sometimes it is helpful to break into small groups of three or four for a while. Shy children feel more free to express themselves in buzzy groups. More children can share ideas in a short time also.

Listening — Encourage the children to listen to others as well as share their own ideas.

Silence — Allow time to think. Silence does not always indicate lack of interest. Sometimes it is a sign that real thinking is taking place.

Conclusion — Discussion need not end in complete agreement. However, when the discussion has been to plan action, aim to achieve a consensus and to have concrete plans made for the next step.

The leader's task is to be clear about the purpose of the discussion and guide it so that a sense of community is maintained. Each individual needs to be encouraged, not allowing one to dominate at the expense of others.

Questions

Questions have a place with every age group.

They can be used to:
— motivate interest;
— focus attention on a topic or emphasise a point;
— find out the level of understanding on a subject;
— accumulate information;
— encourage individual participation.

When asking questions, allow children time to collect their thoughts. Explain that some questions have many answers. If the children don't know the answers, find something positive to say that will encourage further thinking and exploration.

Sometimes it is the leader who has difficulty answering the questions. Seize this opportunity of admitting your ignorance and showing that you too are a learner. Find the answer for them later or suggest how the children can try to find it.

Projects, assignments and learning centres

Children like to discover things for themselves. Here are some ways they can be encouraged to take responsibility for their own learning, to use their initiative, and to spend time on what most interests them and excites their curiosity. Children can work at their own rate, which is helpful in a group with a wide age-range.

Projects
Children can be given sheets with fairly broad instructions, e.g.

The Church Overseas

List Bible references

Tapes

Books

Films

See what you can discover about the Church in another country. Draw a map, make a scrap book, a model or a puppet play to show what you have found.

Work alone or with a partner.

Allow several weeks for a project and conclude with a sharing time together and if possible, interested parents and friends.

Money raising projects
When children have their interest aroused, and they have expressed the desire to help a particular cause, they can be encouraged to raise some money in their own way. The impact of a project will be greater if they choose their own way of working and accept responsibility for carrying it through. Some groups have been successful with bring and buy sales, car wash days, cake stalls or organising shows or film nights.

Assignment worksheets are detailed and specific.

Each child has an individual sheet, attractively set out with illustrations.

A sheet may instruct the children to use a reference book, picture map or magazine to find the answers to questions, solve a puzzle, complete sentences, copy keywords or phrases. Here is an example:

Christmas

Here are 4 things to do.
Choose at least 2.

1. Finish this acrostic with words that remind you of Christmas

   C H R I S T M A S
            T   S
            R   S
            A
            W

2. Paste here a used Christmas stamp

What is the picture about?
Read Luke 2:8-20 and make your own Christmas stamp.

3. Imagine you are one of the shepherds.
   Write to your friend telling what happened on Christmas night.

4. Read the story on the back of the sheet.
   Then make it into a comic strip.

Learning centres

Learning Centres are another way of meeting the questions of the leader who asks, 'How can I reach children who have different interests and abilities?' 'How can I give them more choice about the way they work?'

Several centres equipped for particular activities can be set up.
- a music centre with a piano, percussion instruments, song books and a tape recorder;
- an art centre with paint, paper and scissors etc;
- a drama area with dress-up clothes;
- a reading corner with books and cushions.

The children can move to these centres following input with a story, film or discussion. A sharing time can take place when the large group comes together again.

Following chapters of this book, and books in the reading list, will provide suggested activities for learning centres.

Let's listen to a story

Before you tell a story, make it your own. Read it carefully, noting the pattern of movement. Jot down an outline of events. This will help your memory. Then, knowing the story well, you will be able to tell it in your own words instead of reading. This generally enhances the effectiveness of the story. Note, however, that some stories are designed for reading (and reading aloud at that). No one with an ear for alliteration would dream of putting Kipling's *Just So Stories* into their own words!

Be clear about your reason for telling the story, understanding the part it plays in the session. When story tellers are confident and at ease they tend to increase the dramatic effect by the way their voices rise and fall, their gestures, variations in speed of their speech, confident pauses. However, this skill cannot be forced. It is more important to be yourself, and tell the story honestly, as you feel it. Enter into the story by the power of imagination, and you will find that you can invite children to share the experience with you.

Before you begin, gather the aids you need, your pictures, puppets etc. and organise them in sequence. Telling the story begins when the relationship is established with the children. Let them settle comfortably. Establish contact with the group. Once you have started, discourage interruptions. Nodding at the talker or making a sign to be quiet is all that is needed. After the story children may have some questions. The story may remind them of something they want to tell. Ask your own questions, too, to review the story and check that it has been understood. Encourage several children to speak.

Follow story time with activities through which children can explore and communicate their impressions.

Varying the way you tell the story adds to the interest.
- Tell a Bible story as though it happened yesterday.
- Let puppets tell the story (see later chapter).
- Involve the children in the story presentation:

    Competent readers can read the narrative parts while others read dialogue.

    The whole group can be asked to provide appropriate sound effects as the story is told.

    With a familiar story, children can be involved in many ways, acting it, miming, imagining they were present and being interviewed by a reporter.
- Use pictures. Some stories can be told quite adequately by having a conversation about what the group can see in an illustration, if it is a detailed one. Ask, 'what happened before this?' 'What will happen next?'
- Some songs tell stories.

For extra reading

Refer to pages 92 and 93 for further reading material.

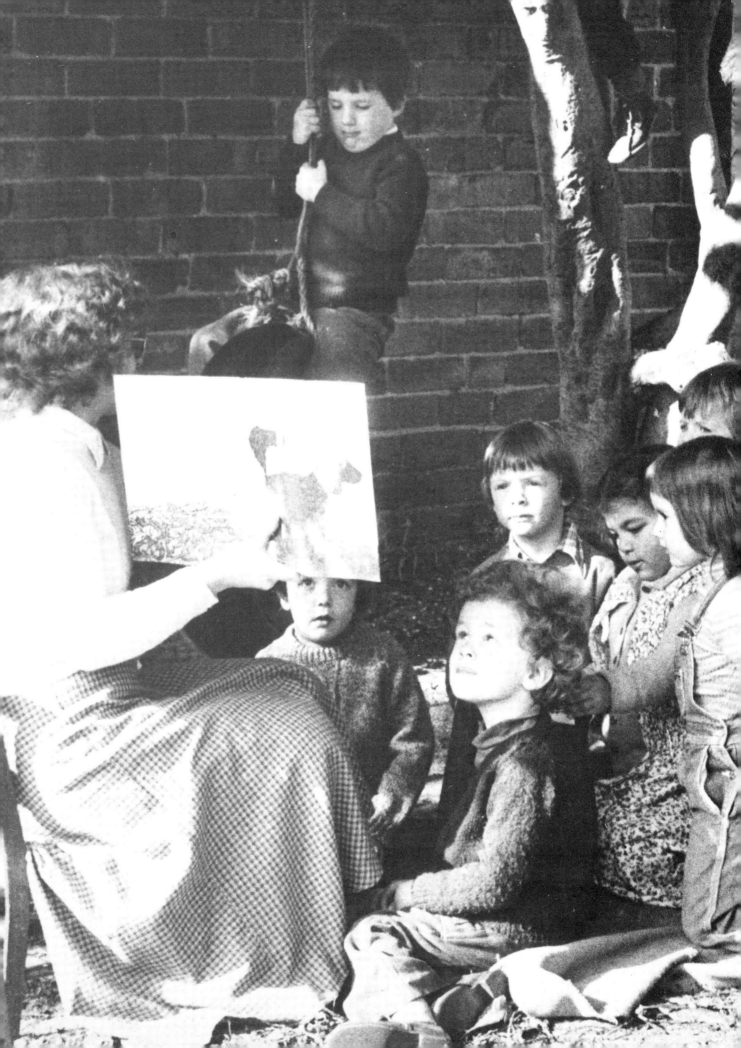

Make a present

for someone in the family. Write a note telling a family member what you like about them.

Cooking

Discuss your favourite family foods. Cook some simple food for your special day.

Stories

Find Bible stories about families.

Compare

the 'past' and the 'present'. Discuss the roles of the people in the family. Ask children to bring photos of their family and extended family.

Role Plays

Children play another member of their family.

Art

Paint 'My Family'. Make 'peg' people of family members. Draw around children on a large piece of paper. Children write about themselves on silhouette.

Special Day

Invite your family to a special party/ picnic or night of entertainment. Play games to help introduce families and group members.

Take a Theme ...
for example

Me and My family

Use your theme as a basis for your activities at meetings or at camp.

Other Themes

- New Life
- Christmas
- Creation
- Friends
- Sharing
- Easter

WHAT I SEE I BELIEVE

Pictures and other things which children can see and touch are amongst the most valuable teaching aids. Seeing and touching for ourselves strengthens our belief and understanding. Pictures, models, puppets, films and objects that can be touched speak as clearly as words — sometimes far more.

Pictures

Keep a useful file:

Pictures from:
- magazines
- newspapers
- photos of the children themselves
- posters
- Sunday school picture sets
- collect children's pictures

Display them:
- set the scene with pictures
- use the children's art work to brighten your meeting place or to initiate discussion

Introduce a new topic or story with a picture. Arouse interest or supply background to a story. Pictures can easily show costumes, buildings, customs and occupations.

Hold the children's interest with a picture as a story is told.

Recall a previously told story — discuss the picture and remember or make a jigsaw.

Represent characters in a story. Discuss how they felt.

Attach speech balloons. Let the children take on the role of one of the people in the picture and suggest the dialogue.

Clarify the meaning of a story with a picture. Children can represent their interpretation of a story with their own illustrations.

Worship — a beautiful or moving picture can contribute to worship or meditation with little or nothing being said.

Flannelgraph

A board covered with felt.

Sets of pictures are available in church book shops or attractive and relevant sets can be made by cutting out your own pictures and backing them with felt or sand paper to adhere them to the board.

Start with a few characters, then include more as you become confident.

Arrange them in order before the story is told. The story teller or children can add or move them when necessary.

Flannelgraphs can be a valuable free time activity or an aid for re-telling a story.

Three-dimensional scenes

Miniature scenes constructed from small models and scrap materials can be constructed on a table, in a box or sandtray to illustrate a story. Children like to be able to handle the figures. Set the scene with twigs for trees and small pipe cleaner figures. Have the basic scene arranged before the children come, then add figures as the story proceeds. Children can recall a story by rearranging the figures themselves.

Diorama

Picture Puzzles

Make your own jigsaws by pasting the desired picture onto a card. Cut into pieces when dry. The younger the children the fewer the pieces. If possible, with smaller pieced jigsaws have a picture for the children to copy.

Overhead Projectors

Overhead projectors offer flexibility, no dark room is required. A file of transparencies can be kept and used for different groups.

Videos and movies

It is easy to capture the children's attention with a film but preparation is needed.

First, ask yourself what your purpose is in using a film or video:
— discussion starter;
— to provide the main input;
— an aid to worship;
— entertainment.

Preview your film — *Is it suitable?*
Time it. Decide how you will use it:
— introduction
— follow-up.

Check the equipment in advance. Make sure that you have everything you need and that it's in running order.

Have you a screenboardpicturehangingbackdropthing?

A screenboardpicturehangingbackdropthing is something every church should have. You can use it for a screen, a chalkboard, a picture hanger or any other backdrop, and you can fold it all away and put it in a corner till next time.

Ideally, it consists of 3 wooden frames with plywood and hessian fixtures hinged together to make a stand up screen. See diagram for suggested size.

I have found this screen an excellent tool for the following uses:
- a screen between groups where there is more than one group in the room.
- a backdrop for a worship centre.
- a handy frame to hang pictures or flannelgraph figures.

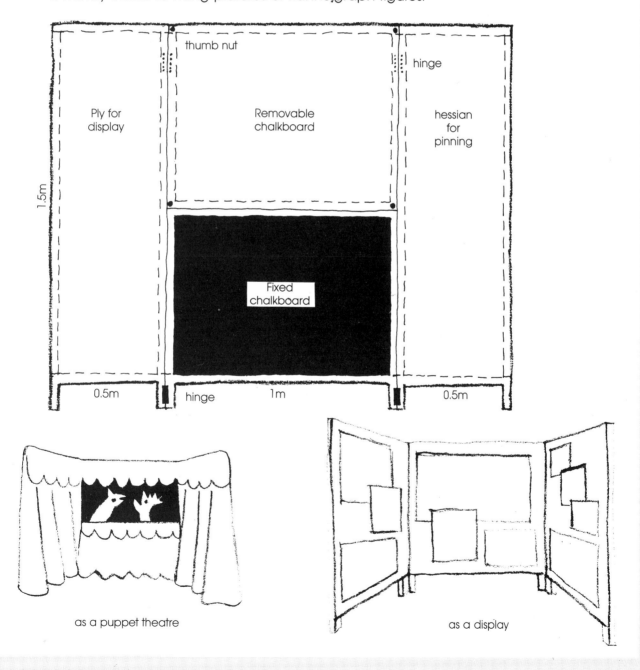

as a puppet theatre

as a display

Let's do it for ourselves

Pictures, films, models and puppets are helpful and delightful, but the real thing makes an even deeper impression. We believe more easily what we can see for ourselves.

- Go on a trip.
- Seeing for yourself how other people live, work and worship is the best way to understand.
- Nature study is all around us.
- Organise a visit to another church or club.
- Walk to the local lake or park. Collect leaves and grasses, or observe birds and animals. *'What can you hear?'*

These activities can be a good introduction to discussions on Creation.

Nature study is all around us

Pressed Flowers

Old telephone books make excellent presses. Slide the flowers and leaves between the pages.

Use them to make bookmarks for gifts or on greeting cards.

Children can make collages with leaves, grasses and flowers.

Growing bulbs is a wonderful activity for children to observe nature at work. Plant late in summer for spring flowering.

Egg cartons are useful for growing small plants from seeds.

Posies make beautiful gifts when visiting sick or old people.

Library visits provide a good opportunity for children to follow up topics which interest them. Bulk loans can provide a supply of books for children's project work.

Walk-in models

Sometimes you and the children can make life-size, or at least walk-in models, either in your meeting place or the church grounds. Use chairs, tables and other furniture draped with rugs or newspaper, cartons, branches etc. to make such things as Noah's Ark, a boat on Lake Galilee, the Temple courtyard or a flat roofed house. The children can sit in their model to hear a story or for worship.

Puppets

Children can make and use their own puppets as described in later chapters. The teacher can also have puppets for use in story telling. Simple stick puppets, bag or glove puppets, or more desirable and expressive puppets with papier mache heads. These can be re-dressed from time to time for use as different characters.

What puppets offer people, especially children, is characters with whom they can relate — warm and loving creatures who show them the gospel of Christ in concrete terms. I have discovered that by using my puppets I can create an atmosphere which is comfortable and 'familiar'. The puppets give out that sense of 'magic' or 'otherness', that charisma, that ability to obtain rapport, which enables them to break into our hearts and speak to us personally, challenging us while at the same time delighting us!

(Know How Book of Puppets, published by Usborne Publishing.)

Cooking and Food

Real food and drink impresses children. Cooking food from another country can be part of a programme involving a slide show and costumes. Children learning about Ruth and Boaz could have a picnic of flat bread and water such as workers shared in the harvest field.

Food is mentioned many times in the Bible. The children could compare the food eaten then with the food we eat now.

Make pancakes on Shrove Tuesday, hot cross buns for Good Friday.

Cooking can be a good way for childen to make Christmas presents. A light meal can be made on a special occasion and parents invited.

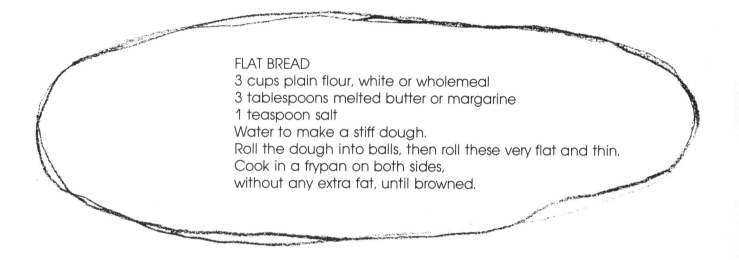

FLAT BREAD
3 cups plain flour, white or wholemeal
3 tablespoons melted butter or margarine
1 teaspoon salt
Water to make a stiff dough.
Roll the dough into balls, then roll these very flat and thin.
Cook in a frypan on both sides,
without any extra fat, until browned.

Visitors

More convincing than stories about people are visitors who can share their experiences of life. Invite people from other countries, people working in useful and interesting ways, people who dance or sing or demonstrate other arts and crafts. If visitors bring objects which children can touch and examine, so much the better.

Visitors need not only be adults, children may benefit from a visit by another group of children their own age. Valuable sharing of ideas could take place during a session involving games, discussions or eating a meal together.

Audio visuals

An audio visual is a set of colour slides with recorded sound to accompany it. Take your own colour slides, or draw directly onto acetate film. Prepare a dialogue or commentary to go with the slides, and record it as described on page 40. Your slides may show the children acting a play, or a series of their own paintings. One group produced an audio visual on John the Baptist with photos of both the children and of art work combined. Another group took the children outside to record their acting of the Easter story. In both cases the preparation was a valuable learning event for both leaders and children. Children enjoyed seeing the result, and these two audio visuals were also quite widely shown to interested viewers.

To make your slides. Collect from your friends any slides they are discarding as failures. Clean off the colour emulsion with bleach. Or you can buy readymounts from a camera shop, in which case you need film to put into the empty mounts. For this, use acetate shirt box lids, or the film used in overhead projectors.

You will also need fine-tipped spirit felt markers (better than water-based felt pens for this purpose), scissors, paper, pencils, a projector and screen. Check the size of the frame in the projector. Some projectors have half size frames which are really too small to work with.

First let children experiment. They can trace some frames onto paper and get used to drawing in this small area. Draw themselves on the beach! Then try on the film. Project this and see the effect.

Now they are ready to illustrate a story. Work with a small group to plan on paper the title, subtitles and pictures you will need. Share out the work, and make your slides. Another group can be in charge of the cassette recorder.

Make your own video

Video cameras can be hired from local schools or community groups to use on a camp or a day of filming activities or a drama session. This form of recording activities could be an interesting basis for an evening of sharing with parents and friends of the group. A trip can be recorded on a tape and used as the starting point for later discussion. See *Drama* chapter for filming guidance.

Adding a MUSICAL dimension

Music adds beauty and richness to our lives. Far back through human history, music has been associated with worship, work, play and the expression of affection and love. Singing and listening to music heightens the spiritual side of our experience. Music can relax tension and awaken a sense of inner joy and well being. It can draw people together in a common experience. Like many other great educators, Plato considered music a basic aspect of education. In *The Republic* he wrote, 'Musical training is a more potent instrument than any other, because rhythm and harmony find their way into the inward places of the soul, on which they mightily fasten, imparting grace ...'

This section deals with background music, singing, making music and movement to music.

Background music

In classes, clubs and camps, background music can be used to help create the sort of atmosphere you desire. You may have a skilled pianist for this, otherwise use records and cassettes. Choose your music carefully, aware of its power to affect listeners. If there is any question of your music affecting other classes or groups, keep the volume low.

- Music makes the atmosphere warm and welcoming for children as they arrive. It suggests community and creates a sense of anticipation.
- During activity periods, especially handcrafts, music covers incidental noises and encourages concentration.
- Before, during and after worship, music helps evoke inner silence and reverence.
- Some music adds to the fun and enjoyment, rouses listeners to more vigorous activity or, when necessary, quietens the atmosphere.
- Used as background music, tunes of new songs you want children to learn gradually become familiar.

Singing

Singing is the 'music of the people', far more than any other form of music. Special skill and training are not essential. Children learn to sing as birds do, by invitation and a natural desire to express themselves.

Choosing Songs

Many collections of songs are available. Check in church bookshops. Multiple copies of a suitable song book could be purchased. Photocopies could be made where there is no copyright restriction. The overhead projector can display the words of songs for a group to use.

Most children memorise songs easily, especially if supported by other strong singers.

Choose songs and hymns for their quality and suitability to the age group and occasion, not just for popularity. Children like familiar songs but they also like variety and are stimulated by something new. Simplicity and directness are also to be looked for. Particularly useful are narrative songs and songs with refrains or many repeated lines. Many Negro Spirituals are suitable. Look for those songs which combine deep meaning or strong feeling with simplicity of expression and repetition.

A group can make up its own songs, putting words to familiar songs.

Keep a list or book of suitable songs for different occasions.

Perhaps the children could list their favourite songs for display so they can remember them when asked to choose a song to sing.

Our Favourite Songs

'Row row row your boat'

'I got a robe'
'Kum ba yah'

Teaching a song

Teaching a song calls for the same careful preparation as telling a story. First, know the song and be ready to give a confident lead, suggesting by your enthusiasm that the song is worth learning. It helps to be able to play an instrument but if you can't there are alternatives:

- tap out the melody on the piano with one finger,
- introduce the song with your unaided voice,
- invite a musical friend to visit the group especially to teach some songs,
- obtain suitable records or cassettes for sing-along purposes,
- ask a musical friend to help you prepare your own cassettes for this purpose,
- ask children who learn the recorder or other instruments to practise a song.

The next step is to stand where all can see you and get the full attention of the group. If children can read, make sure they can see the words. For little ones, you might have a picture that illustrates the song or some actions you have rehearsed. Say a few brief words about the song, and start right in, perhaps playing the tune for everyone to listen. Next, hum the tune together. Children might sing the first or last lines and hum the rest. Try the 'echo' method, singing one line and having children repeat it after you. Do not teach words first and then music; *teach both together.* Sing with the children, but don't let your voice overpower them.

Making music

Children increase their involvement in singing when they can also help to make the music. In addition to inviting help from those who are learning instruments, you can ask everyone to join in with *rhythm instruments*. Older children are able to use them discerningly to beat out complex rhythms, add to the mood of a song, or emphasise key words and lines. Even the young ones need not treat the rhythm instruments just as noise makers. They will get satisfaction from more sensitive use, listening to the rhythm of a song and perhaps tapping it with their fingers before taking up the instruments.

As far as possible, obtain instruments that give a satisfactory sound. Some of these can be home made but others should be bought if funds permit, especially cymbals, bells, xylophone, tambourine, triangle and drum.

Rhythm sticks These are resonant wooden sticks which are held in both hands and lightly struck together. Buy 30 mm dowelling and cut into 20 cm lengths. Sandpaper and stain any colour if desired. Use in pairs.

Triangles If you cannot afford to buy small triangles and strikers, use two large nails. One is suspended on a short piece of twine, and the other is used as a striker.

Sandblocks Are easily made by gluing coarse sandpaper over wooden blocks small enough for the hands of your children to grasp firmly. Two blocks are rubbed together, or a stick can be scraped over one block.

Bells Have several small jingle bells attached to a handle, and a variety of other bells in various sizes. These must be bought. If you have a piece of unused crystal at home, use it to produce a rich bell-like sound when struck with a rod.

Tambourine The home-made variety, constructed from foil pie plates and bottle tops has a certain fun value but is less than satisfactory musically. It is worth buying a few small tambourines. They are particularly satisfying to children.

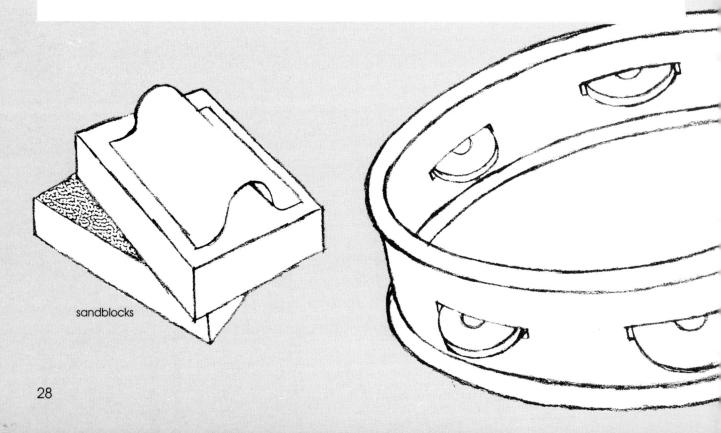

sandblocks

Coconut shells The hollow halves of a coconut shell, cleaned and polished, can be tapped together to make an excellent reverberating sound.

Cymbals Are also immensely satisfying and worth buying. Medium cymbals about 18 cm are recommended, also the small finger cymbals.

Maracas Can be bought, but for a similar effect use plastic bottles in different sizes. Place a small quantity of dried peas, gravel, or sand inside and seal thoroughly.

Drums Avoid tin drums. It is better to have large plastic bottles which can be struck with the flat of the hand. Or make a drum from a small wooden keg, using rubber sheeting, hide or parchment paper to cover the top. Hide and parchment must be soaked in water until soft before they can be stretched over the keg. Attach with large headed upholstery tacks. Start by putting three tacks close together on one side then three more opposite; continue working on alternate sides to prevent the material tearing. Use with the hand or a padded mallet.

These instruments do not make a variety of notes but their different sounds can be orchestrated to highlight the meaning and mood of a song.

Short dry sounds — use rhythm sticks, sand blocks (short quick stroke), coconut shells, tambourine (tapped).

Sustained dry sounds — use maracas, sandblocks (rubbed slowly together).

Sustained tones with greater resonance — use drum, tambourine (shaken).

Tinkling sounds with higher pitch — use triangle (tapped), cymbal (lightly tapped with stick), finger cymbals, triangle.

Ringing sounds — use triangle (quickly and repeatedly struck at one corner or all around inside), jingle bells (shaken for the desired time), cymbals (clashed together), bells.

Collecting instruments promptly after use will avoid some obvious problems.

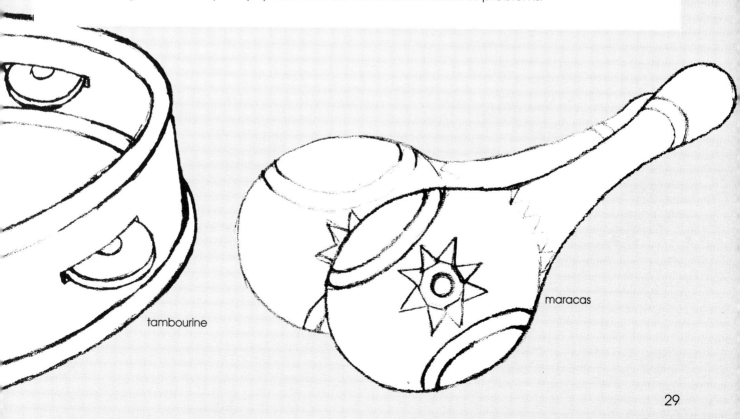

tambourine

maracas

Music and movement

Rhythmic movement is natural to young children and when properly introduced can be one of the most satisfying activities. The objective is to listen to the music or song, hearing and feeling the expressive ideas contained in the melody, rhythm and words, and to explore it with natural movement and imagination.

With little children this can be quite simply achieved either as free expression or as a planned sequence. They enjoy galloping, tiptoeing, walking, whirling and hopping as suggested by the music. They will also express the ideas in a song with more deliberate movements of arms and hands. They enjoy 'action songs' with specific actions for each line.

In clubs and at camp, dancing provides emotional and imaginative release. Try Israeli, Scottish, Maori and other folk dances, square dancing, as well as free modern dancing.

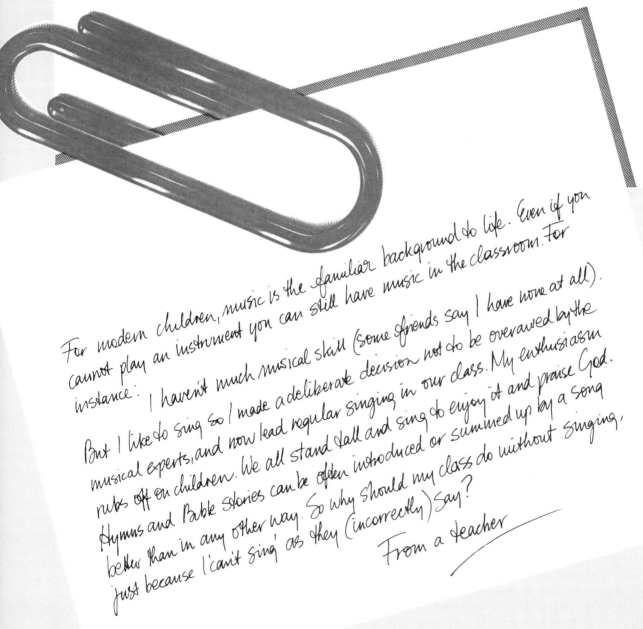

For modern children, music is the familiar background to life. Even if you cannot play an instrument you can still have music in the classroom. For instance:

I haven't much musical skill (some friends say I have none at all). But I like to sing so I made a deliberate decision not to be overawed by the musical experts, and now lead regular singing in our class. My enthusiasm rubs off on children. We all stand tall and sing to enjoy it and praise God. Hymns and Bible stories can be often introduced or summed up by a song better than in any other way. So why should my class do without singing, just because I 'can't sing' as they (incorrectly) say?

From a teacher

ACTING COMES NATURALLY

Drama for children is not 'theatre' as adults see it. Acting is natural for boys and girls. When they are young 'let's pretend' games occupy much of their play time. Drama for children is a natural way of acting out their thoughts and working through new ideas. It may be just experiencing a new situation. For example 'What is it like to be blind?'

The informal conversations and fun that always seem to go with acting make these activities valuable for the growth of relationships between adults and children, as well as between children themselves.

Try some of these ideas:
- Role Play.
- Re-write a story.
- Use art work as backdrops. Music for effect.
- Try a mime.
- Interviews — use a cassette player to interview adults or other children to find out more about the topic being discussed.
- Interview a child actor who takes on a Biblical character.
- Use masks — especially for shy children.
- Invite another group in as an audience if the children want it.

Mime

No words or props are used in the ancient art of mime. The feelings of the characters are expressed silently through movements of the body and expressions on the face. It is the simplest of dramatic arts, but can also be the most demanding, which makes it suitable for use with all age groups.

With young children, try some of these ways of using mime after telling a story —

- Name each of the main characters in turn and ask, 'What sort of person was he/she? Show me!'
- Repeat the whole story, acting out the feelings and movements of characters. Make the movements slightly larger than life. Suggest that children follow your lead, but feel free to improvise their own actions.
- Instead of everyone miming the actions of all characters, children can take parts.
- Children can take turns to mime one character or action. Others guess what the mime represents.

Older children can reflect more on what they are doing. With them you can focus on short key parts of a story. Let them work in pairs, devising ways of showing in mime the reactions and experiences of people, for instance, the parents of Jesus when they found him in the Temple, the blind man when he discovered he could see. Children can perform their mimes for others to see and discuss.

Try this with the group:

Zacchaeus was a little man, but he tried to look bigger by walking on tiptoe. *(All tiptoe around for a moment.)*

People didn't like him, so sometimes he tried to pretend he wasn't there! *(Head down, arms over face.)*

He heard about Jesus and he really wanted to see him, so he ran down the street! *(Run on the spot.)*

Because he was little he couldn't see over people's heads, so he climbed a tree. *(Pretend to climb, arm over arm.)*

Suddenly he heard Jesus call him. *(Hand to ear, surprised look.)*

Jesus said to him, 'Come down!' and he did. *(Climb down, arm over arm.)*

Jesus wanted to have dinner with him, so Zacchaeus led the way *(Hand and arm movements, pointing the way, ushering.)*

Other people grumbled. *(Angry expressions, fingers pointing in condemnation.)* But Zacchaeus was very happy. *(Expressions of delight.)* He poured out his money on the table and told Jesus *(draw out imaginary purse, open, tip it up, spread money with both hands)* 'I'll give back everything to all the people!'

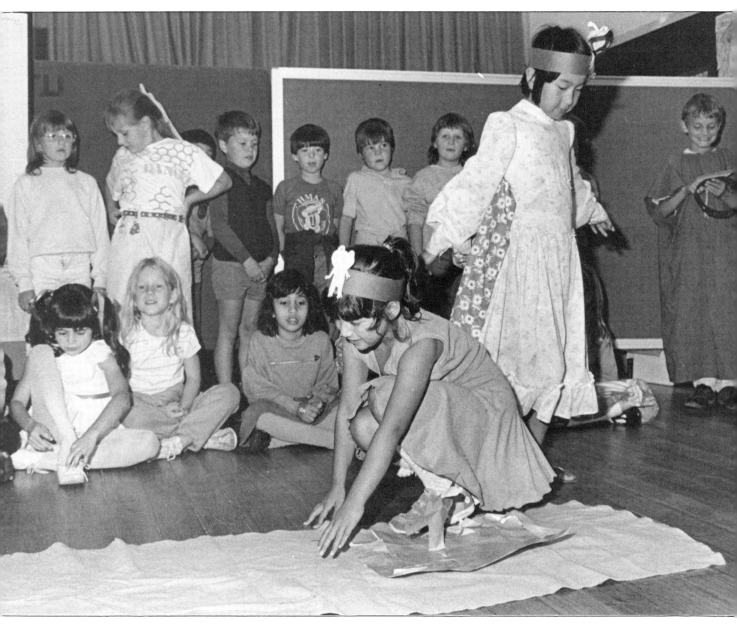

Informal unscripted acting

In the spontaneous acting out of a story, everyone in the group is involved. There is no audience to enjoy the play but the method is of great value to the performers. However, if you want a short play to present, perhaps, in a church service, these informal dramatics can quickly be polished up a little for the purpose.

Follow these steps for spontaneous acting with no prepared dialogue.

Choose the story. Not all Bible stories are suitable. Choose one with plenty of action. If it has a large number of characters, everyone can have a part. If there are just a few characters, the play can be acted several times, with different children taking the parts and interpreting the story in their own way.

Prepare the ground. Read or tell the story, then ask children to recall the main incidents and the characters. With older children, make lists on the chalkboard of the scenes and characters and plan ways of combining, if necessary, a number of scenes into two or three. You need to have done some preliminary thinking about this, as children become impatient with too much time spent on planning. But do not present them with a complete ready-made plan; they need to feel that the play is their own.

Choose the players and other workers. Ask for suggestions or call for volunteers. Avoid stereotyping the sexes, or selecting players because of obvious characteristics. Don't, for instance, ask the tallest boy boy to be king, or a small girl to be a sick child, and so on. As well as actors you may need scene shifters to look after simple props.

Start the action. Don't spend time going over what the actors are to do or say. Let them go! Encourage them to feel that they really are the characters they represent, use their imaginations and throw themselves into the play.

If they get stuck, prompt them with questions such as 'What did the father decide to do next?' 'How did Mary feel about that?'

Afterwards. Talk with children about the play. Ask if they can suggest improvements. Alert them to new possibilities with questions such as 'How could the Hebrews have shown their weariness more clearly?' and then allow a moment for everyone to experiment with ways of doing this. Or if the dialogue strayed too far from the original, challenge the actors: 'Was Charles right when he said . . .?' Let them know that even though they are free to express the story in their own words they should be accurate about the main line and pupose of the story. However, don't spend too much time talking. Let another group of actors have a turn and see what they can do to improve the play.

Costumes. A few simple costumes help to establish the characters in their roles and give atmosphere. For biblical plays the main requirement is for some lengths of striped cloth and a few headbands.

Role play

Role play provides material for discussion of issues and helps children enter into the feelings and motives of other people. Though not suitable for very young children, it is, for children from about nine years up, one of the best methods for relating the Bible message to our lives. Follow these steps:

Identify a problem situation. This may arise in discussion, or you may introduce it as a way of opening up a new theme.

Decide what characters you need to act out the situation and explain that you want actors to behave as they think these people would. They must do it seriously trying to enter into the feelings of these characters. 'To fool is to fail' in role play.

Select persons willing to take roles as they are described. You might describe them yourself or the whole group might talk about the sort of person each character appears to be, or, after giving them the situation, the group of actors, or the individual players can themselves work out their roles. Give each player a name tag, e.g. 'Aunty' or 'Jack'.

Prepare the rest of the group. While the actors take a few moments to decide what to do, suggest that the audience watch out for certain points and how this or that character will react.

Present the play. This should be quite short, rarely more than five minutes. Once the point has been made, step in and cut the action.

De-role the players. Ask players to remove name tags. Ask them how they felt as actors in the situation.

Discuss the role play. Help the audience to think about what they have seen. 'Do you think Aunty was unfair?' 'Was Jack happy?'

Role play is exciting. Because the actors are so fully involved, role play helps them learn about their own feelings as well as the feelings of other people.

With children, avoid choosing situations which would be emotionally demanding, bringing up issues which affect them very personally and cannot be worked through in a classroom. Also, avoid giving them roles which are very similar to their own real life roles: don't ask twins to act as twins or allot the role of an outgoing character to a boisterous child.

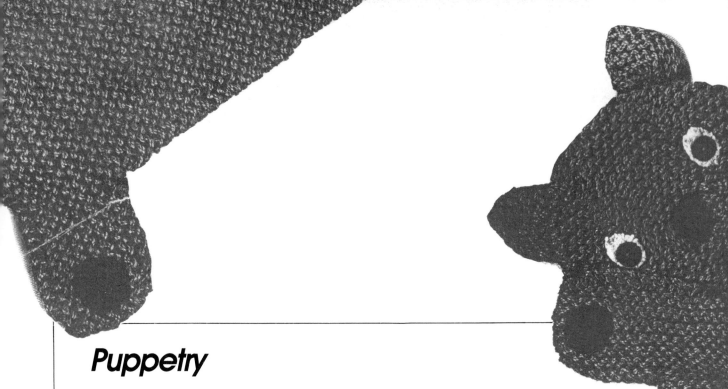

Puppetry

Children are attracted to puppets. They like watching puppet plays and perhaps even more, they like making their own puppets and producing their own plays. Puppetry can involve the whole group. Some children like operating puppets — even those who feel painfully self-conscious about acting will often express themselves freely through the medium of a puppet. Some children find an outlet through other activities associated with a puppet performance: they like to make the puppets, write the script, record it on cassette, experiment with background music and sound effects, or make a stage.

The following steps are recommended:

Choose the story. The most suitable stories have only two or three characters on stage at any one time. The movement should be limited. In spite of this restriction it is possible to refer to large-scale events by having one puppet tell another about them. But avoid long speeches.

Prepare the ground. After reading or telling the story, or outlining the starting point for a new story which the children will make up, decide what scenes and characters are needed, as under 'Informal unscripted acting'.

Allot tasks. Puppeteers sometimes each make their own puppets. Or else while some children make puppets, others write a script, make scenery, etc.

(If you plan to give a public performance of a puppet show, it is a good idea to record the dialogue on tape. Children can then give full attention to the manipulation of their puppets, and voices are not lost behind the screens.)

Act the play and talk about it as suggested for 'Informal unscripted acting'.

Kinds of puppets

Some of the best puppets are made from papier mache (see page 69) but there are ways of producing effective results much more quickly and easily. Even the very little children enjoy making simple puppets.

Stick puppets. A face or even a whole body is drawn on stiff paper or card, cut out, provided with a handle, such as a ruler. Clothing and hair can be drawn or painted or, for a better effect, make clothes from cloth, and hair from wool, string, scraps of sheepskin, etc. Glue these to the cardboard.

Paper bag puppets Use bags about 30 cm by 15 cm. With pastels or felt pens in strong bright colours, children draw faces, hair and clothes.

As a variation, stuff the head with crumpled paper and put a rubber band around the neck. As for stick puppets, additional features and clothes can be glued to the bag.

Glove puppets Choose cloth with a bit of body to it. Cut out the simple shape shown in the diagram, adjusting the size to the hand of the child who is to use it. Machine around the edge, leaving the end open. Turn inside out and make a face with embroidery, applique, felt pen, buttons, etc.

Almost anything can become a puppet — anything you can put a face on — paper plates, fingers, wooden spoons, socks, carrots — well, where does imagination end?

Sock puppet

er bag puppet

glove puppets

finger puppet

Using a cassette recorder

It's fun for children to hear their own voices played back on a cassette recorder. Their interest in the electronic media can be utilised by recording any of their dramatic activities for critical listening and discussion of ways of improving the performance, especially when there is to be a public performance.

The cassette recorder makes possible a whole range of dramatic activities:

Radio type play. Children prepare and record a play. It can then be replayed for class use or perhaps for a church service or other occasion.

Puppet play. Especially when a puppet play is to be given in a public performance, it is helpful to have the sound recorded. Puppeteers can then pay full attention to manipulating their puppets.

Choral reading. Make use of a cassette recorder when preparing a choral reading. When the readers can hear themselves they are able to identify faults and work to correct them.

Mime and interpretive dance. When children are doing movements to a story or song, the sound can be recorded to be replayed as often as needed, while the children concentrate on the movement.

Interview. Simulate a radio interview. Children can impersonate biblical characters and answer questions put to them by another child. Or you may have visitors to the class (overseas traveller, social worker, church member, disabled person, etc.) whom children can question. When recorded, these interviews make interesting listening and stimulate discussion. Help children plan interviews and work out suitable questions.

Practise. If necessary, run through the script before recording. In the case of an interview with children, ask them to answer each question in a 'dry run' to make sure they know what to say. Then turn on the machine and repeat the question.

Record. Hold the microphone 15 to 20 cm from the speaker's mouth, switch on the machine and give a nod to the speaker to start speaking. Turn off whenever there is a break. This will ensure that there are no false starts or awkward pauses.

Replay. Replay at once to make sure you have recorded what is needed. Then your cassette will be ready to use according to plan.

T.V. play. When children make a box T.V. (a roll of pictures drawn on paper to simulate film — see illustration) they can also record an accompanying script, and present a T.V. show with both sight and sound.

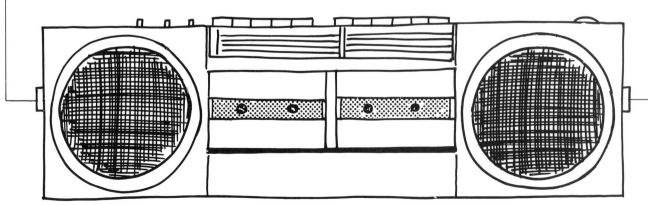

Video action!

Earlier we talked about using video to record events. If you can borrow or hire a video camera there is also the possibility of making your own dramatic films.

Don't be too ambitious when attempting a film. Even a four or five minute production represents a great deal of work.

Consider these issues

Place — Indoors or outdoors? Indoors you need lighting and scenery. Outdoors you need a suitable site and good weather.

Script — Children may wish to write down what they plan to say but it is sometimes more natural for them to rehearse a little first and then just film small segments at a time.

Costumes and Scenery — Make the costumes as bright as possible. Use large paint brushes to paint the scenery on old sheets or large paper.

Work out scenes, characters etc. as in 'Informal unscripted acting'.

Screening — Short viewing sessions can be enjoyed by the group or more polished films can be viewed by parents and friends.

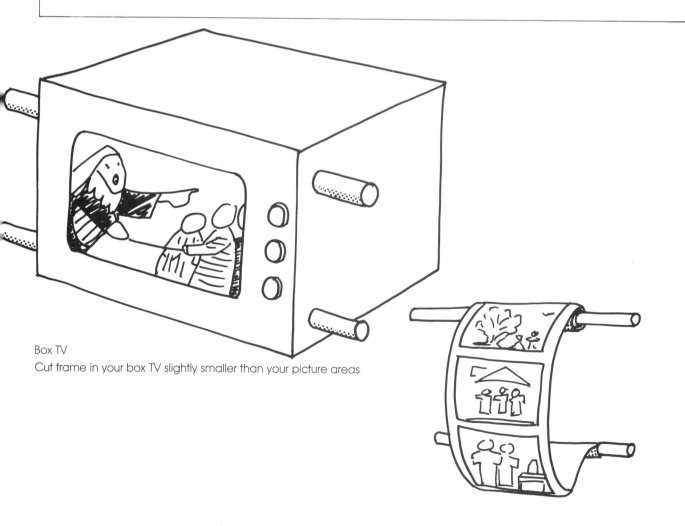

Box TV
Cut frame in your box TV slightly smaller than your picture areas

CHildREN AS AUThORS

Writing individually or in groups helps children sort out their ideas and develop them, check memory and understanding and gives the satisfaction of expressing themselves. Writing skills may vary greatly within a group. You may need alternative activities available, or work as a group with each child providing a page of a book or an illustration.

Imaginative writing usually requires some motivation. They need to have drawn pictures, dramatised, talked together and in other ways thought their way into the theme.

Fun is... By Su.

Fun is a wrinkle,
A crinkle,
A twinkle or two.
A laugh,
A joke,
A pun.
A sparkle, a chuckle,
A trickle of joy.
A trick, come magic,
— That's fun!
A sense of humour is
good to have.
— A limerick, a riddle,
A jest or a jinx,
A grin, a giggle,
A squeaky noise,
A dimple, a smile,
A screech!
Amusement, entertainment,
Enjoyment, delight.
— That's what fun is!

Letters and Cards

Letter writing can be a matter of sending messages of thanks, good wishes, apologies, requests for information etc. as part of the life of the group.

Children can make their own cards for a more personal touch. Or children can write imaginary letters as a way of expressing their thoughts and feelings about a Bible story or life situation:

Dear Joseph,

When I read what your brothers did to you, it reminded me ...

Dear Martha,

I often think about the time when Jesus visited our home. Do you remember....

with love from Mary

The letter form can be a way of telling a Bible story:

Letters can also be a valuable form of communication between the members of a group.

Children can cover a box with red paper and the children and leader can leave letters or notes for each other in it.

Stories

Children may enjoy writing imaginative stories related to the theme they have been working on, or re-telling a Bible story in their own words.

Help the children where necessary by providing an opening sentence or paragraph headings. Perhaps the older children could write and the younger children could do the illustrations.

Write a script for a filmstrip, video or slide set

Working in small groups, children can write a commentary or dialogue to accompany projected pictures. These may be colour slides taken as part of one of their projects, a video of their drama session, or a commercial filmstrip.

Write a 'radio' script

Children can work together on a script in which the story is told by narration, dialogue and sound effects.

Prayers

Some children make their own prayer books, adding from time to time a prayer they have written, or prayers by other people which have an appeal or message for them. Prayers written for use in group worship can be written on newsprint by the leader as the children make suggestions.

The children's prayers could be used in worship with a larger group at a camp or in a church service.

The group could write a prayer or benediction to be used each time they meet and worship together.

Poems

Some children enjoy writing poems and have a real gift for this. When adequately motivated almost all can help compose a few lines with rhythm or imagery, insight or feeling. Even one phrase contributed to a class effort deserves appreciation and recognition. The motivation may come through preparation for a special event or season, or a good story, when children have had a chance to think about it. This work can be done individually or sometimes it is easier to begin with a group effort.

Songs and Hymns

As mentioned in the music chapter, one fruitful idea is to choose a simple well-known tune, perhaps a nursery rhyme or popular song, and set new words to it, perhaps a song of praise or a story in song.

Have this sort of writing done on newsprint so that everyone can see the results and join in singing the new words.

Another idea is to write new verses for a song that is already a favourite.

Newspapers

Can be an ongoing activity in the life of the group. Something to which all group members can contribute. It may reflect a biblical setting (see illustration) or the life of the group. Advertisements for coming events, articles written by children about themselves or people they have interviewed. Newspapers can have pictures with captions, birth, death notices and other public notices, comic strips and leading articles.

A Book

Books can be made with a collection of the children's material — include their stories, prayers, poems, songs and letters.

Other books could be put together by the group over a number of weeks.

A book of favourite recipes could be put together. Completed books could be duplicated and either given to friends or sold as a fund raising effort, or just kept by the children. In one church a fine, well illustrated book was made by children, a one-only copy. It was presented to the congregation in a special offering during a service, and placed in the church library.

An alphabet book provides something for each group member to do.

A is for Apostle B is for Bible C is for . . .

Photo Books

Each child could bring a photo of themselves to be put in a book with something they have written about themselves.

Photos of a trip the children took could be used as the basis of a book.

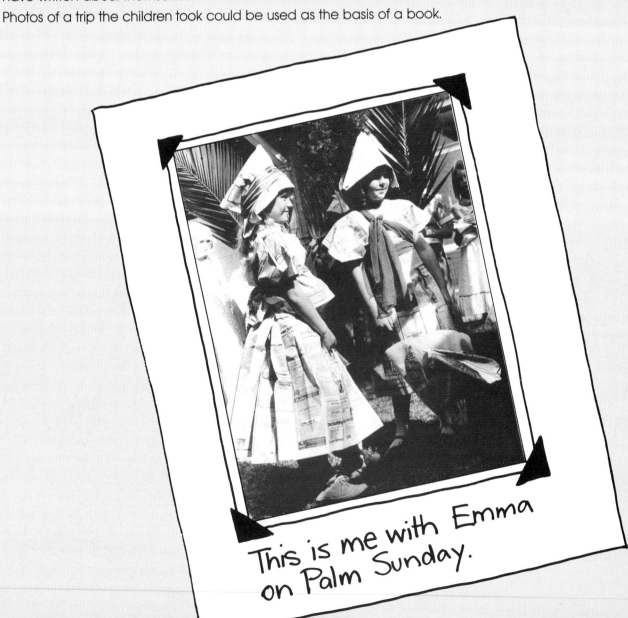

This is me with Emma on Palm Sunday.

Puzzles

Under this heading come all sorts of word puzzles such as crosswords, jumbled sentences and words to unjumble, anagrams and acrostics.

Puzzles can be written on bright cards and kept in a box for children to do when they have finished other activities.

Children can make up guessing games for one another.

Who am I?

**I am a slave,
I ran away from my master,
I met Paul in Prison.**

Coded messages are another enjoyable puzzle game. In one code, numbers are used instead of letters, with numbers 1 to 26 representing the letters of the alphabet.

What is the message?

9.20 9.19 23.18.9.20.20.5.14

Can you spot the six differences?

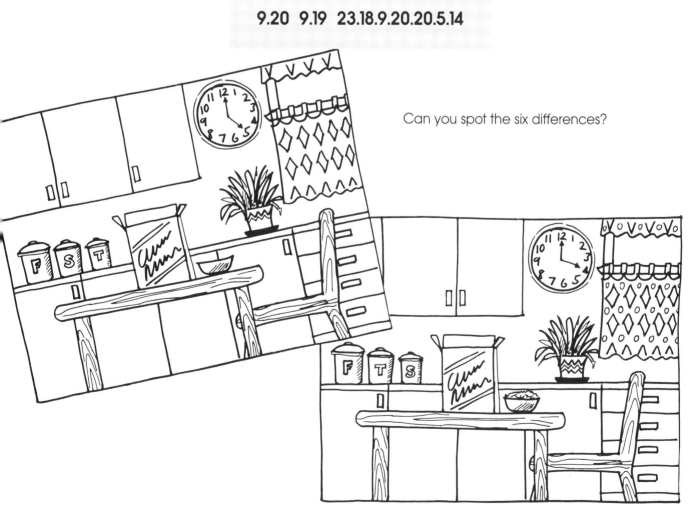

Paint it, draw it, make it, bake it

Everything in our conscious mind comes to us through our senses. How important it is, then, for children to be able to explore the Christian story through handcrafts, activities in which the senses of sight and touch play a large part. Comprehension grows as stories and ideas are expressed with paint, paper, clay, cardboard. In addition, handcrafts add interest, allow the movement which is essential to active bodies, encourage co-operation and give the satisfaction of accomplishment.

Provision of materials and encouragement provide the initial stimulus. The children need to know that they have freedom to express their own ideas, whether working individually or on a group project. This freedom releases them, stimulates them, and helps them to make their own discoveries about their faith.

Recognition of children's work is important. Younger children like to take their work home.

Other opportunities for using children's artwork may arise when making scenery for a play, a mural to show in church, greeting cards for hospital patients, a banner for a procession, or as a way of recalling stories.

Supplies

Here is a list of basic supplies to have on hand for the group to use.

Boxes, glue, wax paper, magazines, cloth, sponges, foil, ice-lolly sticks, feathers, egg boxes, buttons, polystyrene trays, bottle tops, wool/yarn, corks, cardboard tubes, wire, corrugated cardboard.

plus: pens and pencils
     paint and brushes
     paper — large sheets and coloured paper
     paste
     scissors

Have the materials available so the children can choose.

Recipes

Starch paste. Mix two tablespoons of cornflour, powdered starch or plain flour with a little cold water. Add half a litre of boiling water, stirring all the time. The mixture will thicken as it cools. A teaspoon of soap powder will help to avoid lumping. A little antiseptic will slow down mould.

Papier maché. Make starch paste as in the recipe. Put torn newspaper into a bucket and cover with a mixture of starch paste and water. Leave to soak overnight. Next day, squeeze out excess moisture and work with the hands into a firm but pliable dough.

Another method: Use starch paste to build up layers of torn newspaper, tissue towelling or paper.

Modelling dough. Mix five parts of plain flour and three parts of salt with a little water to make a firm dough. If desired, colour with powder paint or food dye. Children may need a little extra flour if the mixture becomes sticky as they work it. Models can be baked in a slow oven. They will then last almost indefinitely if kept dry. Completed models can be painted.

Play dough.

Mix in a saucepan: 1 cup of salt, 2 cups of plain flour, 3 teaspoons of cream of tartar. Then add 2 cups of cold water, 2 tablespoons of vegetable oil and food colouring if desired.

Stir till smooth, then cook over a medium heat until stiff.

Store in an airtight container.

This mixture can be used over and over again, if not allowed to dry out.

Finger paint. Make starch paste as in the recipe and colour with food dyes, powder paint or poster paint. Two or three colours, together with black and white, make a wide range of possibilities. Or put starch paste on the paper and sprinkle dry powder paint where needed, to be worked in with the fingers.

Cutting and pasting

Even before they are old enough to use scissors, little children enjoy pasting paper shapes which have been cut for them, or which they have torn themselves. As skill increases, paper cutting can become more elaborate, even a form of high art.

Paper mosaic

This is a way of making pictures and designs, and is suitable for all ages, and for individual or group projects. You need strong paper for the background, and coloured paper cut or torn into pieces for the mosaic.

Use plain coloured paper, coloured pages from an illustrated magazine, or variations such as crumpled balls of coloured tissue paper. Have the different coloured pieces in separate containers. Sketch a design or outline picture onto the background. Children fill in the outline by pasting on the pieces of paper.

Collage

A wide variety of materials can be used to make a collage design or picture — words cut from a newspaper heading, coloured paper cut into shapes, real flowers and leaves, straw, fabric, feathers and anything else that can be stuck to a background with paste, glue or staples. Pen and crayon lines can also be added. If the collage is a group project, begin by discussing the plan and agreeing on what each person will do. Just to see an interesting assortment of collage materials put out for them to use will set children thinking in original ways.

Newspaper montage

Older children can explore a topic by searching newspapers for pictures, headings and articles which illustrate it. These are assembled in an arresting and artistic format, and pasted to a background of newsprint. Possible topics: 'Who is my neighbour?' 'Lord, we confess . . .' 'Thank you, God, for . . .'

Matchbox   Paper cone   Fold & paste tab to base   3D pictures

Three dimensional pictures

Pictures that stand out from the background, with depth as well as height and length, have interest and realism that children enjoy. Let them experiment with different methods. For a wall picture, objects and figures can be drawn on separate pieces of paper, cut out and attached to the background with paper hinges, or by mounting them first on matchboxes. Or if a picture is to lie flat, cut around three sides of objects and figures that have been drawn; bend on the fourth side to make them stand, as shown in the diagram.

Experiment with other ways of making the picture stand out.

Cut along black lines, fold along dotted lines

53

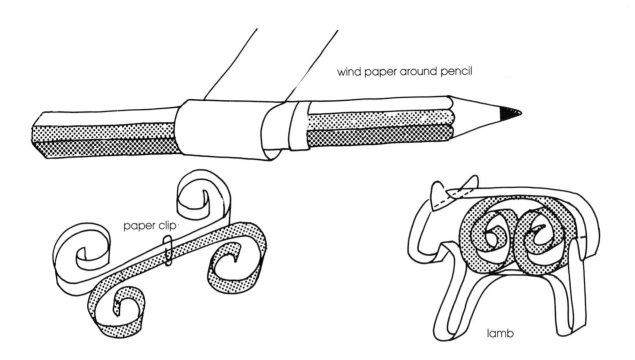

wind paper around pencil

paper clip

lamb

Quilling

This craft may be used for making decorations, Christmas tree ornaments and mobiles. Designs may be symbolic or purely fanciful and decorative. You need long, thin strips of quilling paper no more than 1cm wide, plus paste, scissors and paper clips. Wind each paper strip tightly around a pencil, it will curl nicely. Join the pieces together temporarily with the clips one at a time and paste the parts together. Allow time for the paste to dry.

Once children have seen the method demonstrated they will quickly begin to make their own plans. Use single colours or combinations — perhaps all red for Pentecost decorations, or red and green and white for Christmas. Make a fish mobile to illustrate the story of the miraculous catch, or golden flowers and suns for Easter. For an especially luxurious effect, use gold or silver foil paper.

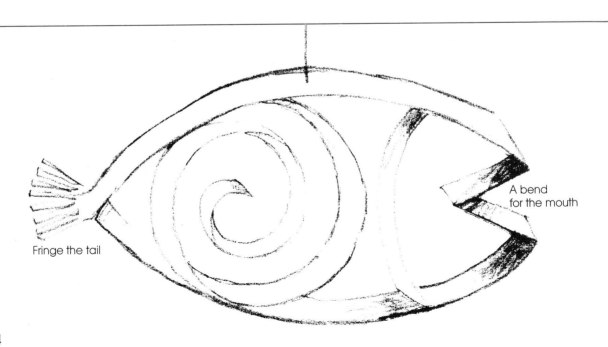

Fringe the tail

A bend for the mouth

Strip of people

To cut out a row of identical paper figures at the same time, take a strip of paper. The size will vary according to what you want, perhaps 50 cm by 10 cm. Fold in half, and then in half again, and again. With the folded edges on top, draw a figure filling the whole length, sleeves going right to the side edges. Cut along the lines you have drawn, but do not cut the edges where the sleeves end. Open up the strip. Draw faces if desired. Paste to contrasting coloured paper.

Make a row of paper children

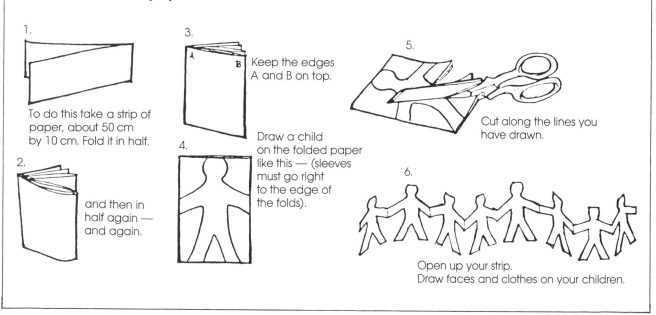

1.
To do this take a strip of paper, about 50 cm by 10 cm. Fold it in half.

2.
and then in half again — and again.

3.
Keep the edges A and B on top.

4.
Draw a child on the folded paper like this — (sleeves must go right to the edge of the folds).

5.
Cut along the lines you have drawn.

6.
Open up your strip. Draw faces and clothes on your children.

Cut or torn figures

Individual figures of people, animals, buildings, trees, can be cut or torn and pasted to paper of a contrasting colour.

Snowflakes

Fold a square of paper in half, then into quarters, and then make one diagonal fold. Clip out small sections along the folds, in the centre and round the edge to make a fancy pattern when the paper is unfolded. Large snowflakes can be used as table mats. Small ones, pasted to paper of contrasting colour, make unusual decorations on greeting cards.

Paperfold cross

Fold paper in half, then into quarters. Tear out the shape of a cross as shown in the diagram. Open up the folds and paste to paper of a different colour. The torn-out corners can be added to the design, if desired. This would be suitable for an Easter greeting card.

Fancy fun writing

Older children especially like doing fancy decorative writing. This cut-out method is intriguing and looks very smart and individual on a greeting card or as a book title. Fold a sheet of paper lengthwise. Use a light pencil to write the chosen word on the folded edge in outline script with linked letters. Cut carefully along the pencil lines through both thicknesses of paper. Open out and paste to paper in a contrasting colour.

Making models

The 'odds and ends box' will be very useful when you are making models. See the list of possible materials at the beginning of the chapter. Children can work on individual models, or help others to make mobiles, decorations, tabletop scenes, or scenes in boxes (diorama, peepshow).

Flat-topped house

For a typical biblical house, use a square of stiff paper with four cuts as shown in the diagram. Draw door and windows, then bend each cut to make the corners of the house and glue into position. Make an outside staircase by folding a strip of paper, and pasting in position.

Paper cut in this way can be used to make a variety of models both square or oblong. Vary the size, texture and colour of the paper, also the depth of the cuts, to make such things as a shallow manger box, a deep basket (add a handle), a swimming pool, etc.

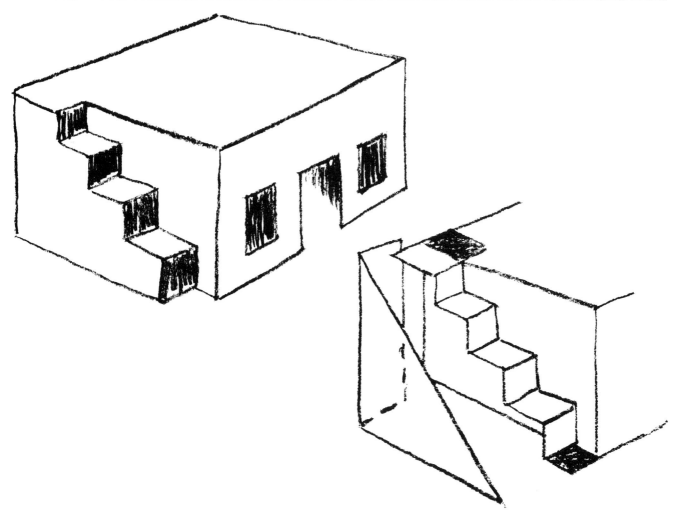

Jack-in-a-box

is fun to make and a helpful way of exploring a story. Older children can make their own boxes. You need a box with a lid; use the bottom of a milk carton or make a cube from card (see diagram). Decorate the sides with pictures or statements about the main character in a story, for instance, 'I kissed my Master', 'I was a disciple of Jesus', 'I took my own life', 'I kept the money bag'. On the lid write, 'Who am I?' Then make a spring from two long strips of firm paper folded as shown; attach one end to the bottom of the box, and on the other end fasten a drawing of the person in the chosen story. Close the lid and pass the box around a group to see who can guess the answer to the question. The one to guess correctly opens the box.

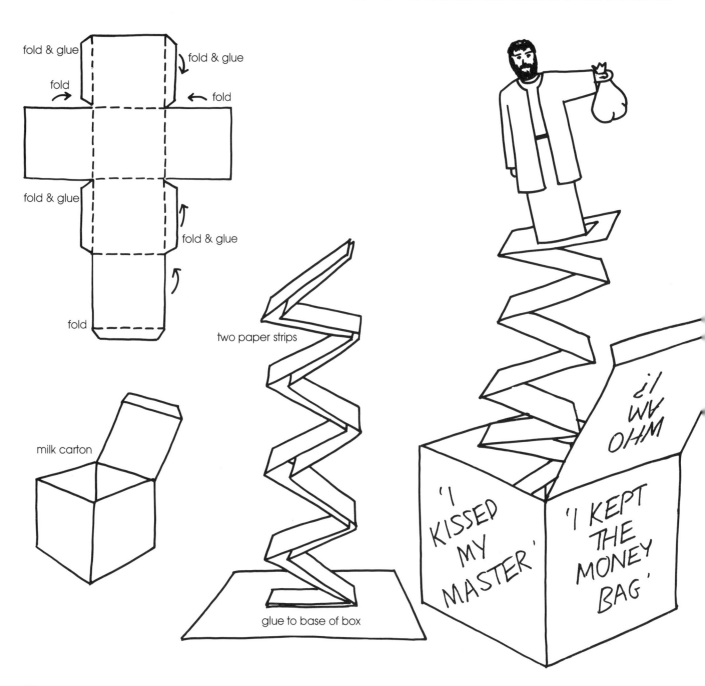

fold & glue

fold & glue

fold

fold

fold & glue

fold & glue

fold

two paper strips

milk carton

glue to base of box

'I KISSED MY MASTER'

'I KEPT THE MONEY BAG'

WHO AM I?

Box story

Take a small box or carton and on each of the six sides paste pictures of one scene from a given Bible story. Children can work on these boxes individually or in groups. They can be used in a game, throwing a box from one to another. Each time it is caught the catcher must tell that part of the story which is uppermost as the box falls.

Pinwheel

For a pinwheel or windmill, fold a square of paper diagonally and cut as shown in the diagram. Draw the four points to the centre and put a pin through them, then through a bead and finally into a wooden handle such as a ruler. Blowing on the blades will make the pinwheel go round. Make them at Pentecost before telling how the Spirit came like a rushing wind.

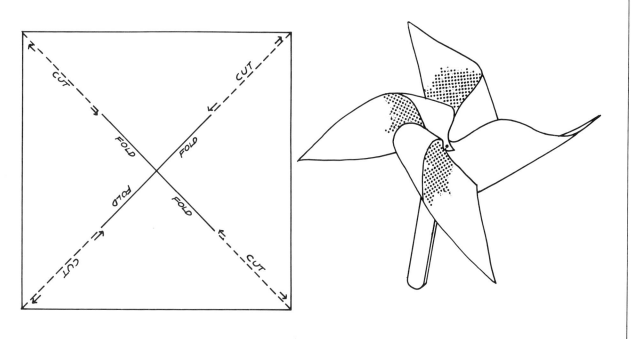

Stars

Two triangles superimposed on one another make a six-pointed star. For a five-pointed star, fold a square of paper in half, then fold again from the centre, slanting as shown in the diagram, so that parts B, C and D are all the same size. Fold B over C and then again over D. Make one cut through the folded paper as shown by the dotted line. Open out the star. To make it three-dimensional, re-crease all folds from the centre to the long points, so that they are all uppermost.

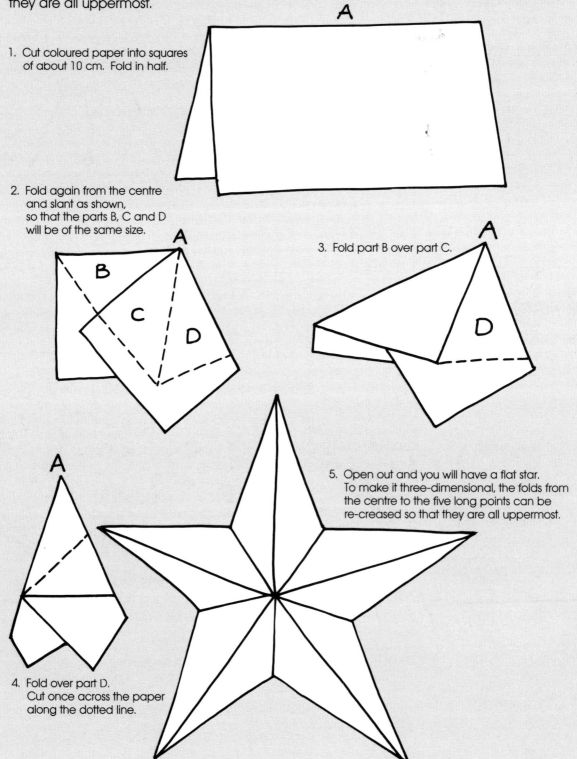

1. Cut coloured paper into squares of about 10 cm. Fold in half.

2. Fold again from the centre and slant as shown, so that the parts B, C and D will be of the same size.

3. Fold part B over part C.

4. Fold over part D. Cut once across the paper along the dotted line.

5. Open out and you will have a flat star. To make it three-dimensional, the folds from the centre to the five long points can be re-creased so that they are all uppermost.

Cone figures

A circle of paper with one cut from the outside edge to the centre is the basis for a number of useful models. Diagrams show how it can become a tent, a mountain, a container for sweets. It can also become an angel by adding face, arms and wings, or without the wings, any sized person.

cone for sweets

tepee

cottonwool

snow-topped mountain

ping-pong ball

cotton wool hair

Palm leaf cross

These crosses are often made by children and distributed to worshippers in church on Palm Sunday. They are best made from strips of palm leaf or other thin, flexible leaves such as Iris, but can also be made from strips of quilling paper. See diagram.

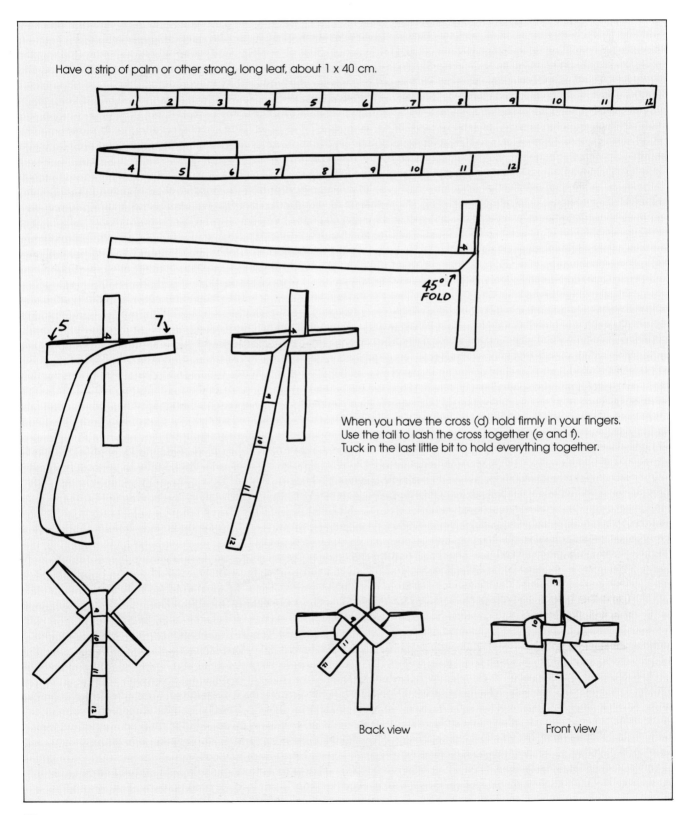

Have a strip of palm or other strong, long leaf, about 1 x 40 cm.

45° FOLD

When you have the cross (d) hold firmly in your fingers.
Use the tail to lash the cross together (e and f).
Tuck in the last little bit to hold everything together.

Back view

Front view

Birds

are symbols of the Holy Spirit,
of God's care as shown in the story of Noah, of peace and of
cheerfulness. The two basic styles shown here can be varied in size, decoration and colour.
Hang paper birds from a thread in a window, on a tree, or use in making a mobile.

The body is cut from light card.
The wings are made from light paper folded
accordion- fashion, passed through
a slit in the body.

This strip-paper dove is less realistic and may appeal to older children. Cut a sheet of
paper into about twelve strips, about 1½ by 20 cm. Fasten with a staple at one end to
form the head, snipping the edges to make a beak. Fasten at the other end to make
the tail, first layering the strips as shown in the diagram.

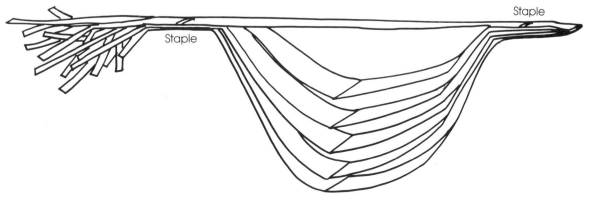

People and animals

The diagrams show a variety of methods for making small models which will stand up. These few examples will suggest many other possibilities.

Old-fashioned wooden dolly pegs, if available, are speedily transformed into people. Make clothes from scraps of fabric secured around the waist with rubber bands. Make faces from paper pasted to the head. Make stands from clay or dough.

Pipecleaners are easily twisted into the shapes of people and animals. Buy fluffy coloured pipecleaners.

Figures of trees, people, animals, buildings etc. can be drawn on card, cut out, and fitted with stands.

pipe cleaner animals

Tin can lantern

It's fun hammering nails, and children will like making these lanterns at Easter, Christmas, Pentecost or other time when light is an important symbol. The punched designs on the lanterns can be varied to express the theme.

You need canned fruit tins or tins of similar size with the tops neatly removed. Fill with water and freeze solid. Draw designs on the tins with felt pens. Then, using hammers and large and small nails, punch holes along the pen lines. Melt out the ice and fix candles inside the tins, using clay or melted wax. Tins can be painted black, but in the dark you will only see the sparkling points of light.

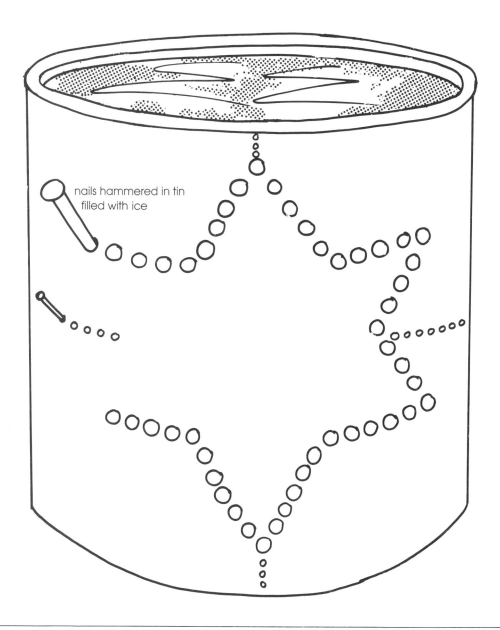

nails hammered in tin filled with ice

Modelling and sculpting

A most satisfying activity for all ages is working with the hands, kneading and moulding clay. Commercial or home-made modelling dough, bread dough and papier maché are similarly valuable. You may need protective floor covering and overalls for the children for modelling activities.

Modelling dough

See recipes, page 50, for salt dough and a boiled dough that can be re-used again and again if stored in an airtight container. Salt dough models can be baked in a slow oven, then painted; they almost have the permanence of ceramics.

- Salt dough stars for Christmas decorations can be moulded by hand or cut with biscuit cutters. Before baking, insert small hangers made from florist's wire. After baking in a slow oven, paint and sprinkle with silver glitter.
- Salt dough beads have the holes made with a knitting needle before baking. Paint them when they are cold.
- Many small articles made with dough can be useful for dioramas and table models.

Clay

In some areas you can dig up all the clay you need, but generally it is best purchased from an art shop or educational supplier. If you plan to use it frequently, buy a quantity but make sure it is properly stored in an airtight container such as a large ice-cream box or rubbish bin with a close fitting lid.

Before it is used, clay needs 'wedging', that is, banging on the table to remove air bubbles.

Encourage children to pound and squeeze the clay before they begin to make anything. This renders the clay more pliable and helps young artists to feel more free, too. This manipulation is in itself a way of self expression and has value even if nothing else happens.

Models are best made from one lump of clay rather than from small sections joined together as these tend to fall apart as the clay dries.

Even if clay models are never fired they will last a long time, so long as they are kept dry.

A way of storing clay

Plastic cover or shower-cap

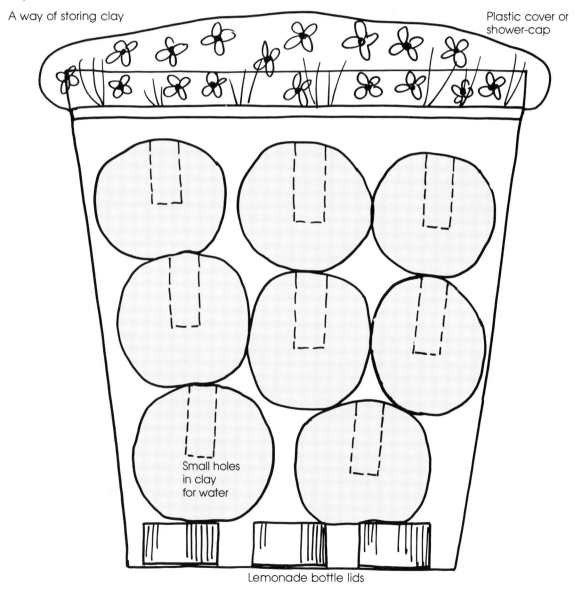

Small holes in clay for water

Lemonade bottle lids

Bread dough

Bread dough stands up well to the vigorous working which children usually want to give it. If you only have a short time, make your dough at home from a standard bread recipe. Bring it to your group after the first kneading and rising. Give children small lumps to work on. Bake their rolls or models if you have an oven at church; otherwise children can take them home for baking.

- Apart from the parable of the yeast, many Bible stories refer to people eating bread together. As children work on their dough, explain the way yeast works, and how important bread is to most people of the world.
- If making bread for Holy Communion, children can shape their rolls into cross shapes, circles, or sheaves of wheat. (The ears of wheat are made by snipping the dough with scissors.)
- Hot cross buns for Easter have spice and currants added to the dough. The crosses are made from a stiff mixture of flour and water, rolled thin and cut with a knife or shaped with fingers.

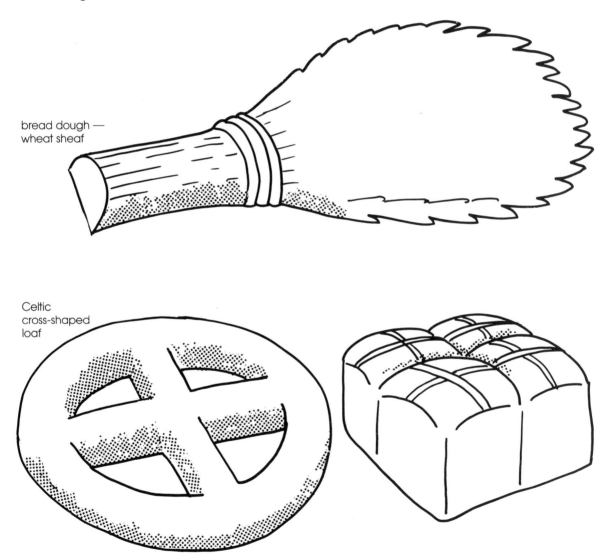

bread dough — wheat sheaf

Celtic cross-shaped loaf

Papier maché

See recipes, page 50. This material is excellent for making relief maps, masks, heads of characters in stories, pinatas, and many small objects required for acting and models.

- **Relief map.** Use papier maché to build up the map on a board. First draw the outline on the board and mark in areas for mountains, rivers, etc. so that you know which parts to have high and which to keep low. When the papier maché is dry it can be painted in traditional mapping colours, with names printed in black.

- **Mask.** Use a mould for this. The outside of a pie dish or plate is suitable. Grease it well with fat or oil so that the finished mask will not stick. Cover completely with three or four layers of paper and paste, or with mashed papier maché. Use extra material to build up eyebrows, nose, chin, cheeks. You can even roll strands for hair. Allow several days for drying, then remove from the mould, paint the face, trim the edges and add ties.

Pinata. Make a pinata in much the same way as the head, with a balloon as the basis. A popular treat at party time in South America, the pinata is filled with nuts, sweets and favours. It is hung by a strong cord to a tree or perhaps a rafter in a hall. Taking turns, children are blindfolded and given a stick with which they try to break the pinata. This is not easy, but great fun. At last it cracks open! The contents fly out and everyone scrambles for a share.

Unlike the head, the pinata must have an opening left at the top so that it can be filled. It must also have a 'harness' so that it will hang securely. To make the harness, first cover the balloon with three or four layers of paper. Then wrap it with cord or strong nylon string like a parcel, leaving the ends tied at the top for the hanger. Cover the string with several more layers of paper. Leave to dry before painting or decorating with frills and streamers of coloured paper, projecting horns etc. to make it as fantastic as possible. If the balloon has not already collapsed, puncture it now and fill the pinata.

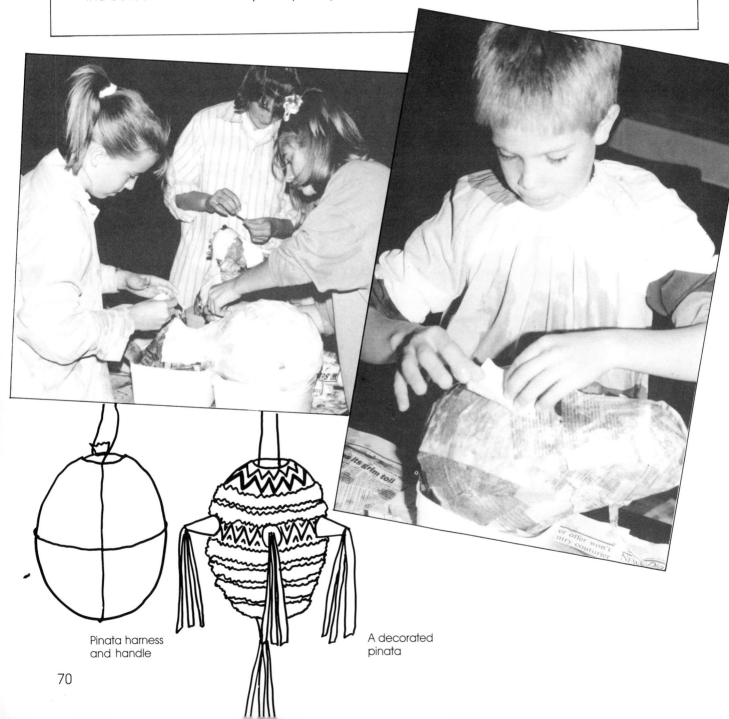

Pinata harness
and handle

A decorated
pinata

Puppet heads. Unlike paper bag and many other simple puppets (see page 38) those made from papier maché are very durable and can be moulded into subtly realistic or bizarre features. It takes time and dedication to the task, so is not recommended except for camps or perhaps a series of craft sessions in a club. Mould the papier maché over a ball of loosely crumpled newspaper, or better still, over a mould made from clay.

When dry the papier maché is cut in half vertically and the clay removed. Then the two sections are rejoined with extra strips of paste and paper. Make a 'collar' round the neck from a twist of paper and paste to form a ridge that will hold up the clothes. Insert a tube of card into the neck for the puppeteer's index finger. Stitch felt hands to the puppet's sleeves; these are like gloves and have a cardboard tube in each one for the operator's thumb and middle finger.

For a larger puppet head, blow up a balloon and cover with papier maché, using strips of paper and paste. To keep an even thickness, use alternate layers of white and coloured paper. Build up features as for the mask and leave hanging to dry. Then paint the face and make a wig, from wool, strips of paper or cloth, steel wool etc.

DRAWING AND PAINTING

Most children enjoy working with pencils, brushes and chalks, though a few feel self-conscious about it and retreat with the familiar complaint, 'I can't draw!' Understanding leaders help these children join in by adopting a warm but matter of fact approach. They may assure a child that the standard of drawing does not matter, though this line is not always successful. Or they may suggest an undemanding task such as painting in solid colour for sea or sky in a group project. There is usually some way for shy children to share with the rest of the class in the satisfaction of a completed project. They may be willing to do the lettering for a poster or paste leaves to a collage tree. They will prefer unskilled activities until their confidence develops. They will feel safer with materials that do not call for fine work — finger paint, large-headed brushes, thick pastels used on the side. First, then, what materials are needed?

Paper

Large sheets of paper encourage a bold and confident approach. Newsprint is adequate for most purposes, but a glazed paper is better for finger painting. For a change, try coloured paper, with just one or two contrasting coloured paints or pastels.

Paint

Powder paint and ready mixed poster paint are more economical when bought in the larger sizes. Let children blend their own colours from a basic range of red, yellow, blue, black and white. Put out small quantities at a time in jars or saucers. Put powder paint into egg cartons; children can dip wet brushes into the dry powder. For finger paint, see recipes, page 50, or buy ready prepared.

Brushes

Have long handled, broad-headed brushes. For older children have some finer brushes as well. Make sure brushes are treated carefully. Bristles should not be squashed into the paper but used with a brushing movement. They need to be thoroughly washed after use and stored in a jar with bristles uppermost.

Pens, pencils and crayons

Felt pens are expensive and quickly dry out but they are useful at times, especially for lettering on a poster. For young children the most satisfactory media are oil pastels, wax crayons and soft, thick, black pencils. For older children have oil pastels, coloured pencils, ballpoint pens and felt pens.

Art projects can be large community affairs, or small and individual. Beginning with the large scale projects on which several children can work together, here are some examples of activities that will encourage co-operation, help build friendships, and develop a sense of community. Large works are impressive and increase the feeling of achievement, as well as being effective in communicating ideas to larger numbers of people. As in other types of handcrafts, there is value in 'thinking big'.

Poster

A poster is a bold, easily grasped design which conveys a message. It can use a combination of words and illustrations which should be simple and strong in colour so that they can be seen from a distance and easily read. Use the minimum of words, or at least have the key words standing out in plenty of space. Children can make posters to advertise coming events such as a special family or children's service, a fund raising event, or a club meeting.

Triptych

A triptych is a screen with three panels hinged or joined together. A triptych can vary in size from a one or two metre high screen that stands on the floor as a room divider or scenery in a play, to a small focus of attention on a worship centre. Make panels of cardboard, wood or even stiff paper. Tops can be arched, straight or rounded. In each panel have one scene or symbol related to one common theme, for instance an Easter triptych with scenes showing Palm Sunday, Good Friday and Easter Day. A repetitive border round each panel will give unity to the whole.

A diptych is similar, but has only two panels. It stands like an open book.

Mural

A mural is a large picture painted on a wall or displayed on a large area of wall space. For our purpose it is any large picture which illustrates one or a series of stories, or which shows a development of ideas around a single subject. Use paint or oil pastels, perhaps in combination with collage materials. It is practical to have some children doing the background, while others work on smaller pieces of paper doing sections of the work, perhaps individual people, flowers or buildings, which they then cut out and paste in position on the mural.

Especially when painting, it is often best to work with the paper on the floor. Before beginning, discuss with the group what they want the mural to show and what media will be most effective. Decide who will be responsible for each part. You might need to keep a list of these decisions.

Triptych

75

Frieze

A frieze is a long, narrow strip of pictures or designs to display around a wall. It could show a series of scenes, such as the seven days of creation, or a series of people, such as the twelve disciples or the ten sick men. Or it could consist of a repetitive design such as butterflies, stars, leaves.

Scenery

Making screens and hangings as scenery for even a simple play gives the opportunity for involving children in addition to the actors. Paint scenes on large sheets of paper, or draw on old sheets or curtains with wax crayons; iron the work with a hot iron and the wax becomes imprinted. Costumes can be decorated in the same way.

Cartons

All six sides of a large carton can be covered with newsprint and then with children's paintings and drawings. Six aspects of a story, or six stories in a series, can be displayed on one carton. Several cartons stacked in a corner look quite decorative.

Banners

The best banners are made from cloth. They are long-lasting, and when carried in a procession have an eye-catching swing and movement. If only to be used once for a particular occasion, a paper banner, too, can be really impressive. A procession with banners proclaims a message about the meaning and importance of the occasion to those who are watching. When children make and carry banners in a church procession, this is an emphatic statement about their place in the congregation.

The design of a banner needs to be simple, bold and uncluttered so that its message can be quickly grasped. A cloth banner can be decorated with embroidery, appliqued designs either stitched or pasted in position, paint, fringes. Whether paper or cloth, a banner needs one or two poles for bearers.

'Stained glass'

Drawings made on cellophane with felt pens can be displayed in a window where they give the effect of stained glass, especially when strong black lines are included to simulate the lead in a real stained glass window.

Let children closely examine some church windows before they try this medium, noticing the technique of combining small sections of different coloured glass with lead strips, and painting details onto the glass.

For another method, draw the picture on plain white paper and colour the design thickly with oil pastels. Lay the picture upside down on newspaper and rub all over with vegetable oil. A few days later apply a second coat of oil, leave to dry. Fix into a window with sticky tape.

For both these methods, make sure the paper is cut to size so that it will fit into the window where you plan to display it.

When children work on their own individual paintings and drawings, make sure that it is appreciated. Display it on pinboards or screens. Peg the papers onto a string stretched across the room or between two chairs. Look at one another's work and encourage children to talk about what they have done.

Sometimes individual work can be combined, for instance, as pages in a class book. Bind pages together with stitching, staples, or cord, or hinge pages together to make an accordion book.

Accordion book

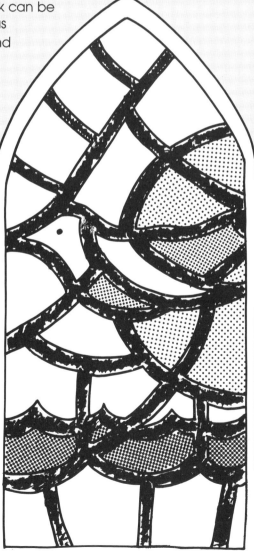

Rebus

A rebus is a picture-puzzle story in which the words are represented by pictures. They are fun to make up, the children will also enjoy trying to read the ones their friends have made.

Read this:

Read this: (peas) $t + ter had a (boat) on the (water)

He took Jesus to (cat) + ch some (fish)

(wren) w + they pulled in the (net)

it was full of (fish) Jesus asked Peter to follow him

and go (boat) for (people)

instead of (fish)

Comics

Comics are another form of picture story, one that most children find irresistibly attractive. Here again, they can make their own.

Buttons

It's popular these days to wear buttons that show where your loyalties and interests lie. Apart from designing buttons and having them made commercially, which is expensive, look out for materials which can be used to make your own buttons. Cardboard and firm plastic on which you can write with felt pens are obvious suggestions. The important thing is to decide on the words and/or pictures.

Cards

There are frequently opportunities for children to paint or draw on small cards for greetings, invitations, notices, etc.

Eggtree

Egg decoration

Easter is the special time for decorating eggs, either hardboiled (for younger children) or blown (for older children). Decorated eggs are given as gifts, hung as a mobile or used to make an egg tree, which is a beautiful and symbolic addition to church or home at Easter time. Draw on eggs with felt pens or dip into dye for plain bright colours.

Older children are capable of experimenting with batik methods. Basically, this involves making a design with wax, for example, drawing on the egg with a light coloured wax crayon or a white candle. The egg is then dipped in dye. When dry, the wax is removed by holding the egg beside (not over) a candle flame, then wiping off the wax with toilet tissue as it melts. The design then appears in white on the coloured background.

To blow an egg, pierce each end with a skewer or large darning needle. Hold over a dish and blow strongly through one end. Use yolk and white for cooking. Rinse the shell and allow to dry.

To hang an egg, tie a section of match stick to a thread and push through the hole at one end. Pull lightly. The match will turn sideways and will not come out.

Printmaking

Print making is a craft which can be used occasionally, especially with older children, when a large number of identical items are needed. For programmes, greeting cards and invitations, handcraft printing gives an attractive and relatively quick result.

Potato cuts

Cut a potato to give a flat end about 5 cm in diameter. Draw a design on this flat surface. It needs to be very simple, so that the surrounding potato can be cut away from the outline, leaving a raised design. Use a penknife or woodcutting tool for this.

Make a stamp pad from felt or a piece of cottonwool cut from a roll. It must be flat. Place on a plastic lid or flat plate and moisten with poster paint, or dampen slightly and sprinkle with powder paint, working this in to get the desired depth of colour. The pad must not be too moist or the prints will smudge. Practise on spare paper before attempting the final print.

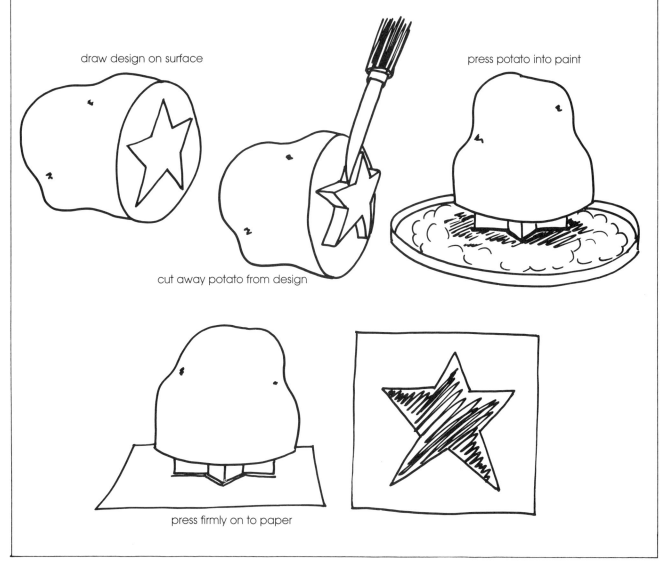

draw design on surface

press potato into paint

cut away potato from design

press firmly on to paper

Sponge or cork printing

Use small pieces of plastic sponge held in clothes-pegs and print with these in the same way as potato cuts. Without attempting to make a variety of shapes, the sponge can be used to give interesting effects and is easy for young children to use. Experiment also with different size corks.

Leaf prints

Use the same style of stamp pad as above. Select small leaves with interesting outlines and strong ribs. Press a leaf firmly onto the stamp pad and then onto paper. Lay another sheet of paper on top and press down firmly with the palm of the hand or a roller. Lift top paper and leaf carefully to avoid smudging. A number of leaf prints can be made on one sheet of paper. When dry, select the best, cut them out and paste to the clean card or paper which they are to decorate.

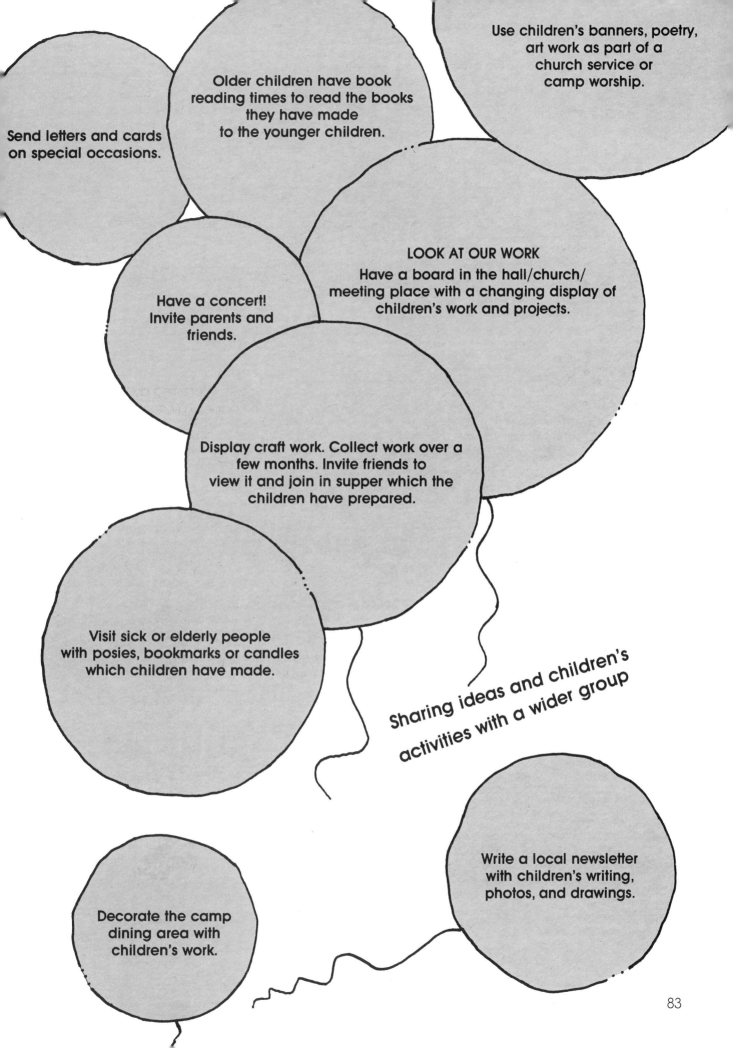

Send letters and cards on special occasions.

Older children have book reading times to read the books they have made to the younger children.

Use children's banners, poetry, art work as part of a church service or camp worship.

Have a concert! Invite parents and friends.

LOOK AT OUR WORK
Have a board in the hall/church/ meeting place with a changing display of children's work and projects.

Display craft work. Collect work over a few months. Invite friends to view it and join in supper which the children have prepared.

Visit sick or elderly people with posies, bookmarks or candles which children have made.

Sharing ideas and children's activities with a wider group

Write a local newsletter with children's writing, photos, and drawings.

Decorate the camp dining area with children's work.

WORSHIPPING TOGETHER

Christian people come together to praise God, seek his help, learn to know his way for us and, even more, learn to know him. This is worship, an unusual activity in our present society. What else that we do is quite like it? Yet more than anything else about church life, worship is what binds Christians of all ages into a community, the unique community of the body of Christ, the family of God. Children value worship. Nevertheless, they often find adult services boring and confusing. Even services planned to include children all too often fail to do so.

Planning for children's worship

When ministers, and others responsible for children's worship confer together, seeds of new thought may be sown, even though immediate changes may be difficult to implement. A good beginning is to consider the children who actually are in the congregation. In the average church, some of them will still be non-readers, or very slow readers. They may not be able to read most of the hymns, even children's hymns, or join in responsive psalms and prayers. They cannot comprehend abstract religious language and do not have the language themselves to express their own faith, which is often sincere, complex and profound. The senses of sight, sound and feeling are of even greater importance to them than the adults. They respond to sounds such as the organ, brass bands, bells. Their attention is caught by the sight of banners, pictures, flowers, vestments, processions. They warm to the feel of hands as in the passing of the peace, and the reassurance of parents and friends sitting close beside them in church.

Groups of children might prepare a contribution to the worship of the congregation. It might be planned as part of their weekly meetings or at a camp.

It could be an excellent way to share the work of the group with the adult congregation.

Worshipping with the congregation

Children can contribute to worship in many ways, therefore making it more meaningful for them.

Children's prayers, drama, artwork, and songs add to the warmth, interest and meaning of a church worship time.

Families can contribute as a group by
— making a banner
— writing and reading a prayer

Worshipping in your own group

Worship in a children's group

should
- be short and informal
- be part of the whole topic a group is working on
- involve children personally through their active involvement
- express group fellowship and help build community
- give opportunity for children to speak to God and listen to him.

At Camp

Worship can take place early in the morning or as a way of bringing the group together at the close of a day. Children or families can worship together in different ways if they are outdoors.
— singing and praying around a camp fire
— celebrating the seasons
— celebrating nature and studying nature first hand.

With a group of children or families together at a camp it is an excellent opportunity for the children to participate in worship. Prayers, stories, songs and Bible readings can be linked with the theme of the camp.

Songs

When choosing songs, look for those that are:

- easily read or quickly memorised by the age group in question;
- written in modern language, keeping clear of abstract expressions and difficult theological words on the one hand, and sloppy sentimentality on the other;
- about situations and issues that have meaning for the children;
- set to tunes they enjoy singing.

When new songs are to be learned, do not teach them during the worship, but make time for this before or after the session.

The thankyou song

From God Gives . . . Songs for kids, Book 2. JBCE. Used by permission.

Words and music Students and Teachers of the Westbourne Pk.Uniting church middle Primary Sunday School dept.
arranged by Ann Parker

Prayer

Prayers should be short and, as far as possible, involve children in their preparation or presentation. For example:

- Relate prayers to the session topic, extending the theme into a new dimension of thanksgiving, confession, intercession.
- Have prayers with responses, making sure that the responses are suited to the reading level of the children or their ability to recall and repeat them.
- Ask children to compose prayers for use in worship, either complete prayers or sentences in a longer prayer. Write on chalkboard or newsprint so that all can join in.
- Invite spontaneous prayers from the group, perhaps just a word or two, as when children make suggestions for thanksgivings or intercessions. Many children, when they feel free of pressure from either leader or other children, will contribute sentences or even whole prayers with insight and sincerity.
- Prayers are often printed to be read in unison. These will be less formal if children have a moment first to read them silently and think about the meaning, ask questions about them, select words and phrases in the prayer which seem to them especially important.
- Relate prayers to pictures and other visuals, especially those made by the children. For instance, if they have made a mural of 'Jesus the healer' everyone can look at this during prayers of thanksgiving for health or intercessions for the sick.
- Echo prayers, when pupils repeat each phrase as the leader says it, is a method often used with little children, but can be equally valuable in helping older boys and girls to focus attention on a prayer and make it their own.
- Excellent prayers for children can be found in Prayer books in the 'Extra Reading List'.

Familiar prayers. Some prayers are part of the common heritage of the church, a sign of unity and a source of strength when we say them together. Children like being able to join in. You may spend time memorising prayers, set them as 'homework', or use them so regularly that they are memorised without effort. Having words on a poster so that they are learned correctly. (Everyone must have heard of howlers such as 'Harold be thy name' and 'Lead us not into Thames Station'.) Use the form of words used in your own church, consulting your minister. Even when other set prayers are rarely said there is always the Lord's Prayer and Benediction and perhaps some other verses so frequently used that everyone is expected to know them by heart.

Opening responses:

This is the day which the Lord has made.
We will rejoice and be glad in it.

OR

The Lord be with you.
And also with you.

Let us praise the Lord
Thanks be to God.

OR

Lift up your hearts.
We lift them to the Lord.

Let us give thanks to the Lord our God.
It is right to give thanks and praise.

tween sentence prayers:

Father, hear our prayer.
Through Jesus Christ our Lord.

OR

Lord, hear our prayer.
Lord hear us.

Praise:

Glory to God, Father, Son, and Holy Spirit:
As in the beginning, so now and for ever,
Amen.

Benediction:

Go in peace to love and serve the Lord.
In the name of Christ, Amen.

OR

The grace of the Lord Jesus Christ, and
the love of God, and the fellowship of
the Holy Spirit, be with us all evermore,
Amen.

The Bible

Almost always the Bible will be used in worship, or at least it will be clear that it is the source of a story or verse that is used. It should be clear to children of all ages that the Bible is a special book, of central importance to the church. Using the Bible in a variety of ways increases interest and involvement.

- Echo reading is like echo prayers, when children repeat each phrase after the leader. Sometimes, with younger children, words can be accompanied by mimed actions.
- Dramatic reading. When a Bible passage includes some dialogue, children can take parts and read dramatically. Have a narrator to read the sections between the dialogue. Sometimes a play reading is available, based on a Bible passage.
- Film strip or movie. A vivid visual presentation on film helps to make a Bible story live, so long as the quality is acceptable.
- Movement. Expressive movement to the music of the words.
- Acting. Free acting of a Bible story by children has special value. See Drama chapter.
- Puppets can be used by either leaders or children to tell a story.
- Pictures and models. Their own work or that of other artists can be used to help children recall a Bible story in worship.
- Memory work. When children memorise Bible verses, ask them to repeat these in worship.
- Choral reading. A group can practise reading in unison, and then present their choral reading as part of worship.

Silence and meditation

Here personal involvement in worship is often at its greatest. Many children value silence and can be encouraged to use it well by a leader who has and who seeks an inner calm. Suggest silent reflection on a song, a picture, one short phrase that arises from the learning experience. Silence is also part of guided meditation, when the leader goes through a Bible story, for example, suggesting that children imagine themselves to be actually present at the scene. For meditation, begin by asking children to sit in a disciplined, aware position with eyes closed, either cross legged on the floor, or erect on a chair with feet together and hands loosely in the lap. Help them focus their minds by concentrating attention on their breathing, or heartbeat, or on the small sounds around them. Then recall the story, speaking slowly with long pauses. Conclude with a moment of silence before asking if anyone has anything to share about the experience.

Meditation usually gives a sense of peace and joy, but may occasionally allow hurt feelings or a sense of guilt to come to awareness. A child may need to talk this over with the leader.

Further reading and resources

General
Working with Children in the Church (NCEC).
A fully illustrated training book designed to encourage and stimulate those working with children in the church community.

Leading Children in Faith video (NCEC in conjunction with Church of Scotland Education)
to be used in conjunction with *Working with Children in the Church* (NCEC).

All God's Children, a hard hitting report commissioned by the Church of England general synod. Essential reading for those concerned with children's evangelism.

John M Sutcliffe, *Learning and Teaching Together* (Chester House Publications).

Go for Six (NCEC).
Bible based material for holiday clubs and all-age events in the church.

Talking and doing
Bible reading material for children (The International Bible Reading Association).

A Yearful of Stories (NCEC).
Suitable for reading aloud to children of about 3-11 years old.

Noelene Martin, *Moving Mountains* (NCEC).
Faith stories suitable for reading to children of middle school age.

Worshipping together
Come and Praise (BBC Books).
A BBC radio collection of contemporary and established hymns.

When you Pray with . . . series (NCEC).
Contemporary prayers specially written for use with children and young people.

Acting
Putting on a performance (Scholastic Publications Ltd).
Another title from the Bright Ideas Series.

Ann Thompson, *In on the Act* (NCEC).
A drama workshop handbook.

RADIUS (Religious Drama Society of Great Britain) plays (NCEC).
A variety of short plays and sketches published in conjunction with RADIUS.

Paint it, draw it, make it, bake it.

Bright Ideas (Scholastic Publications Ltd).
A whole series of books providing a wealth of ideas for use in children's groups.

Violet Philpott and Mary Jean McNeil, *The Know How book of Puppets* (Usborne Publishing).

The books recommended on pages 92 and 93 are available from good Christian Bookshops, or in case of difficulty from the National Christian Education Council, Robert Denholm House, Nutfield, Redhill, Surrey RH1 4HW.

YOUR good ideas!